Best wishes to ✓ W9-BFA-022
near double

Closing Doors, Opening Worlds

Looking Beyond the Retirement Horizon

Vern Drilling

Vern

DEACONESS
PRESS
MINNEAPOLIS

Library of Congress Cataloging-in-Publication Data

Drilling, Vern.
   Closing doors, opening worlds : looking beyond the retirement
horizon / Vern Drilling.
        p.   cm.
   ISBN 0-925190-63-2 (pbk.)
   1. Retirees—United States—Life skills guides. 2. Retirement—
United States—Psychological aspects. I. Title.
HQ1063.2.U6D75   1993
306.3'8—dc20   92-45063
                                                                     CIP

Published by Deaconess Press (a service of Fairview Riverside
Medical Center, a division of Fairview Hospital and Healthcare
Services), 2450 Riverside Avenue South, Minneapolis, MN 55454.

Cover design by Peter Hautman.

First Printing: March, 1993
Printed in the United States of America

97 96 95 94 93   7 6 5 4 3 2 1

Publisher's Note: Deaconess Press publishes books and other mate-
rials related to the subjects of physical health, mental health, and
chemical dependency. Its publications, including *Closing Doors,
Opening Worlds,* do not necessarily reflect the philosophy of Fairview Hospital and Healthcare Services or their treatment programs.

*For a current catalog of Deaconess Press titles, please call this
Toll-Free number: 1-800-544-8207.*

Table of Contents

About the Author   *iv*
Author's Note   *v*
Foreword   *vii*
Introduction   *ix*

1. When the Rules Change,
   You Need a New Game Plan   1

2. All At Once I Was Somewhere Else!   13

3. Start Rockin' Right Now   41

4. How Did I Get Here? Why Am I Here?   55

5. Being Somebody   91

6. You Can Be What You Always Wanted To Be   113

7. Opening to a New World   129

8. Dangers Along the Way   143

9. Managing Employee Retirement
   for Fun and Profit   159

10. Approaching Autumn   169

About the Author

Vern Drilling is president of LaMancha Corporation, a consulting firm that helps organizations manage change through applied behavioral science. He has been a counselor and consultant for over twenty-five years, starting in 1967 with Pioneer House, a Minneapolis chemical dependency treatment center. He joined the Johnson Institute in 1970, where he worked as a counselor, trainer, and consultant. Since 1973, he developed an international employee assistance program for Cargill, Inc., a multinational company with approximately 50,000 employees worldwide. He managed this program for eighteen years.

He has counseled, lectured, and presented training seminars in Europe, South America, Australia, and southeast Asia. He holds a bachelor's degree in psychology from the University of Minnesota, and also did graduate work in psychology at that institution. He has authored several monographs on the cross-cultural aspects of social issues, and since 1975 has conducted retirement-planning seminars and counseled individuals before, during, and after retirement.

Author's Note

I've been fortunate to know many people who have struggled with mid-life crisis, career change, retirement, and other changes in their lives. They came to me for counseling, and I often learned more from them than they learned from me. I'm grateful that they were willing to share what they had learned from their experiences. The best way I can repay them is to try to pass on this learning to others.

The paragraphs in this book that are in *italics* are the personal reminiscences of these people. Many prefer to remain anonymous, and it would be impossible to give proper credit to everyone. Therefore, I've only identified them by age and gender, to give you some reference point.

Closing Doors, Opening Worlds is dedicated to all those who were willing to share the knowledge they gained as they went through their struggles. Their positive outlook on life, and their faith in themselves and in the ultimate goodness of people, should serve as a model for us all. I am especially grateful to the memory of Wally Dean, my counselor, friend and mentor, whose gentle wisdom I have tried to pass on to others.

Foreword

When a company reorganization forced me to take early retirement at age fifty-eight, at first I was devastated. I felt rejected, useless, and lost. But it was the greatest opportunity of my life. It forced me to take a look at who I was, what I wanted out of life, and what I really wanted to accomplish. If I had stayed on that job, I would have coasted along peacefully through security to senility. I would have never known what I was missing. I'd been a living case of mistaken identity. I thought I was a job description, but found out I was a person.

When I walked away from that job, I closed a door and opened up a whole new world.

(Sixty-three-year-old man,
five years after retirement)

Most people in our society get much of their identity, self-worth, feelings of accomplishment, and satisfaction from their job or profession. But each year, millions of Americans change jobs, quit working, or retire. There are books, training sessions, and counselors to help them find a new job, change careers, or find better ways to sell old skills to new employers. But they're left unprepared for the most profound changes of all—the changes in feelings of identity, of knowing who they are and where they want to go.

If you're facing retirement, job loss, career change, or what today is called mid-life crisis, this book is for you. It will help you prepare for the emotional and social readjustment that is needed to successfully adapt to such a major change in your life. It will help you anticipate the changes, identify your goals, and develop strategies for changing perspectives, activities, and relationships. You'll be prepared to manage change, rather than be managed by it.

It will help answer the question, "Where do I go from here? And where's *here?*"

Introduction: A World You Weren't Prepared For

I don't suppose that anyone remembers what it feels like to be born, although I've heard that some people claim they can remember the experience. But it must be an awful shock. Nine months of feeling safe, warm, protected, and secure. Completely familiar with your surroundings. Everything the same, even feeling your mother's heartbeat. Then all of a sudden you're pushed out into a cold, bright, noisy, strange and threatening world, kicking and screaming. A world you weren't prepared for.

I think I've learned what that feeling is like. With thirty years in the same comfortable, safe surroundings on that job, I knew what to expect. I didn't realize just how secure that feeling was. And then all of a sudden I was pushed into a strange and frightening world. Of course, I kept quiet because I'm a grown-up. But I'm kicking and screaming inside because it's so different from what I was used to, and what I expected.

But just look at little kids a year after that birth trauma. They're not afraid any more. They've

adjusted, they're happy, and wonderfully curi-
ous, always getting into things. Every day's a
new experience. And why are they so happy?
Because they're learning and growing.
Well, I'm a lot like those little kids. I'm happy
and excited about life, too, and I'm having new
experiences every day. I'm learning, growing,
and playing. But those kids start from day one,
and I wasted about three years. I wish I had
started that learning and growing a long time
ago, long before I retired. It would have made
retirement more fun right from the start. And
I would have enjoyed my years on the job more,
too, if I knew what I know now. So you see, for
me, retirement has been a lot like birth. I guess
you could call it a rebirth. I just wish I had
started sooner, and I wish I hadn't gone through
that awful period of feeling so lost and confused.

(Fifty-eight-year-old retired man)

"A world you weren't prepared for." That captures the
feeling I've heard expressed so often in the twenty-five years
I've been counseling people before, during, and after their
retirement. You'd think they'd be prepared, wouldn't you?
They knew it was coming, they even had a good idea when.
We plan for everything else in life, don't we? Why aren't
people ready for this one?

I thought I was prepared. I'd made some finan-
cial projections. They weren't as rosy as I'd
hoped, but it looked like we could be pretty
comfortable if we were careful. We'd talked
about where to live, and finally decided to stay
right here. It made the most sense financially,

and we'd be close to people we knew. Besides, we like it here. It looked like there'd be enough money to spend a month or so in Texas or Arizona in the winter. I thought I'd find plenty to do with my time. It seemed like I never had enough time to do the things I like. Now I would.

That's what most people talk about when they're planning for retirement, things like finances, where they're going to live, and what they'll do with all that leisure time. Those are important issues, and they should be on everyone's list. But there are other issues that are equally important, ones that may affect you even more than finances or where you live. People work their whole lives looking forward to retirement, and then when they face it head-on, they're afraid. Why? Because the issues they face are different than the ones they expected. They're caught unawares. They weren't prepared for what happened.

I didn't think much would change, and the changes I did expect were pleasant to anticipate—more time, less stress, things like that. But boy, did things change! It snuck up on me because it involved parts of my life that I thought would stay the same. And the change was subtle, so it was going on quite a while before I realized what was happening. I just knew I didn't like it. Something wasn't right, but I couldn't put my finger on it. I didn't expect so many things to change, and I didn't expect it to hit me so hard.

Change is usually stressful, but you've been dealing with it all your life. So what's so stressful about retirement? It's a *major life change,* and that kind is always traumatic. The fact that most people aren't expecting it to be quite so major probably adds to the trauma. Believe me, it is major. If you accept that, you'll be ready to devote the planning and energy it will take to make your retirement successful.

I Wish I'd Known Sooner

Change can bring disasters, or it can provide opportunities. The bad news is that nearly every retiree I've talked with has had to grapple with at least some of the problems described in this book. The good news is that most of them were able to manage the change successfully. But nearly all of them say that they wished they had known sooner what to expect. They wished they had been better prepared to retire. They would have made fewer mistakes, avoided wasting time, and got on with enjoying life.

> *Retirement was a rebirth all right, but it sure was a long and painful labor. Tell them not to hide their heads in the sand. It's going to be tougher than they think. I hope someone else can learn from my mistakes!*

Many people simply avoid thinking about retirement or aging. They go on with their lives as if nothing will ever change. This is called *denial.* In its milder form it's something like, "Oh, that's a long way off. I'll start thinking about it a couple of years before I retire." I've had some people tell me, "It won't happen to me. They can't force me to quit at age sixty-five anymore. I like what I'm doing, so I'm just going to go right on working. Besides, I can't afford to retire." About the only part they got right was that last part.

Sometimes the denial is total. I once had a woman in my

office the day of her retirement party. She had spent her whole working life with the same company. "I know it sounds crazy," she said, "but I totally blocked it from my mind. My job has been my whole life. I somehow fooled myself into thinking that this would never happen. I don't know what I'm going to do."

Sometimes the denial is subtle. "It's going to be just wonderful! I'll be able to do all the things I ever wanted to do." For many, retirement *is* wonderful, but only if they've anticipated the problems and planned how to meet them. It's going to happen whether you're ready or not. Be ready.

You'll notice that there won't be much "psychological" talk in this book. I'm not going to pretend I'm an expert who can give you a solution to every problem you're going to face. No one person has all the answers. During the last twenty-five years, I've counseled hundreds of people as they've approached retirement or gone through other major life changes. I'll try to pass on the accumulated wisdom of those people, because they've lived through it and learned from the experience.

As so often happens, they came to me for counseling and I learned more from them than they learned from me. You can learn from them, too. How often have you said, "If I knew then what I know now?" Well, this is a chance to use what *they* know now. I think they'd all be happy to know that someone else benefited from their struggles.

When the Rules Change, You Need a New Game Plan

The Need for Personal Restructuring

Trevesco Corp. announced today that they are planning a complete restructuring of their operations. "It's not that we're in trouble," said Robert Williams, the chief executive officer. "We've been very successful in most of our product lines, but the business climate is changing rapidly. We've got some great talent and some real strengths, and we want to be sure we're making the best use of both. We think we can do that by applying that talent to some new and developing markets. We've always had high standards, and we're certainly going to keep those. We're just going to apply them towards new and better goals."

Personal Restructuring—You're the Architect

You hear a lot these days about corporate restructuring. Facing a changing world, companies realize that they need to take a fresh look at what they're doing, and make some changes if they want to continue to be successful. They rethink their mission, what they are trying to accomplish, and what kind of rewards they expect. They set new goals. Then they assess their strengths and weaknesses and decide how to apply them to the new mission. They eliminate some old practices and introduce some new ones. They capitalize on their strengths and try to improve areas where they are weak.

We all face a changing world, and if you're likely to be retiring in the next ten years or so, it's going to be changing even more than you expect. So doesn't it make sense to think about *personal restructuring?* Apply the same principles that work for business to your life. Decide what's really important to you, what you want to accomplish, and how you want to live the rest of your life. What kind of rewards do you want? What are your strengths and weaknesses and how can they best be used to get what you want? Determine what stands in the way of reaching your goals, and decide what you have to change or improve to get there. Try to anticipate what you must do to adapt to changes along the way.

Of course this process makes sense, but it will work better if you have some guidelines to help you with the restructuring process. A business usually calls in an expert consultant to help them decide what resources need to be strengthened, eliminated, or changed. You can rely on the most expert consultants of all, those who have done it and learned from the experience. The people who have been most happy and successful in retirement shared some characteristics during their years on the job. As your consultants, they'll tell you that these are the strengths that helped them the most:

• They had a realistic idea of their strengths and weaknesses.

• They set high standards for themselves. They measured

their progress against their own standards rather than the opinions of others.

• Their identity was not tied to their job, but rather to their spiritual beliefs and moral values. Most had an active religious affiliation.

• Throughout life they had devoted time and effort to improving themselves.

• They were involved in leisure, social, and volunteer activities during employment; their job was not their whole life.

• They were team players. They liked working with others towards a common goal.

• They were able to define their interests and what they wanted out of life.

• They enjoyed using their skills in service to others.

• Though not wealthy, they were relatively stable financially; there was balance between their income and their lifestyle.

• They learned to become flexible; they anticipated and planned for changes in their lives.

That's a good list of basic attributes for you to consider. How do you stack up? This book will help you in the restructuring process and suggest some strategies to start strengthening the areas of your life that need it.

Our consultants are also in agreement about what you can expect. First, they'll tell you that it's normal to be a little apprehensive. In fact, it's healthy, because it means that you know there are going to be some hurdles to overcome if you're going to be successful.

The issues you need to anticipate and analyze as you go about your personal restructuring can be grouped into three categories—changes, opportunities, and dangers. Obviously, you need to be prepared for the changes, be prepared to make the most of the opportunities, and be forewarned of the dangers, so that you can avoid them. Let's take a closer look at these issues.

Anticipate Change

I never dreamed so much would change. I thought I just wouldn't be tied to a work schedule any more. But I found that retirement caused changes in all kinds of things, things that had been stable before.

The changes that you'll encounter as you enter retirement will be more profound than most of those you've faced before. There will be more of them occurring at once, and they'll affect areas of your life that have been relatively constant in the past, such as relationships and daily activities. The way you manage these changes can have a big impact on the way you think and feel about yourself. Here are some of the things you need to start preparing for:

Change in structure. Much of your daily life is now molded within a certain structure. You go to work at a certain time, come home at a certain time, and do many of the same things every day. You don't have to give much thought to what you're going to do next. Some activities are so predictable that they could almost be called rituals. Removing that structure can be a great experience, freeing you to do more of the things you like. But it can also have some negative effects, and might leave you feeling bewildered. It's as though you went through life following a road map, and now the map is gone.

Change in how you feel about your place in the world. Your job, your profession, and being part of an organization are ways in which you feel that you are a part of something larger than yourself. There are other ways too—family, church and community, for example—but in our society, the job is usually one of the most important. You're going to have to find other meaningful ways to make your connection to the world.

Changes in identity and self-worth. Much of your feeling about being a worthwhile person comes from what you accomplish, from the recognition or the feedback you get from others. There are many ways of achieving a positive identity, but you've probably become accustomed to getting much of it from your job. Without it, you might have some trouble figuring out just who and what you are.

Changing relationships. Association with others on the job is an important part of social life for many people. When they retire, they think that these relationships will remain the same. They usually don't. Your relationship with your partner, friends, and others will change, too, as your daily activities change.

Loss. There will be losses, both positive and negative. You'll lose some of the restrictions that may have prevented you from becoming the person you wanted to be. There will also be losses that are hard to accept. You'll lose some sources of identity and satisfaction, power, prestige, or control that may have come with your job. Recognition from others, social interaction on the job, and the feeling of being part of a team will have to be found from other sources. You'll likely lose more friends and loved ones to death or geographical moves as you grow older, too. Many of these losses can be anticipated, so plan ways to replace them with other sources of satisfaction. And the most difficult, such as the loss of a loved one, can be easier to accept if you've fully developed your personal and spiritual resources.

Anticipate Opportunities

Along with these changes and losses, there will be exciting new opportunities, and if you're prepared, you can take full advantage of them. Some people keep most of their old activities and old associations because they truly enjoy them. But many see this new freedom as a chance to live a very different life.

> *It's a totally new lifestyle for me, almost completely different than on my old job. These days I put all my energy into doing things I always thought I would have chosen for a career if I hadn't had to worry so much about financial security. I'm tutoring kids and I have a paid part-time job at the school as a teacher's aide. So it's really a job, a second career. It ties me down a bit, but it's worth it. I like it a lot more than my first career, and I get a greater feeling of accomplishment. I wish I had started on it earlier.*

(Sixty-nine-year-old man)

People who are successful and happy in retirement usually say they took advantage of several different kinds of opportunities. In addition to pursuing avocations or second careers, these are the ones most frequently mentioned:

Opportunity for new relationships. Different activities, a more flexible time schedule, and the pursuit of new interests will bring you together with different people who share those interests and activities. Some of them might be very different than your current friends. Usually people associate with others who are very much like themselves. That can lead to a narrow view of the world. Making new friendships is a way to learn more about the world and about yourself. This can be especially true if you have the opportunity to make friends with people from other cultures and backgrounds.

> *I haven't given up on my old friends, and hope I never do. But through my church, I got involved with sponsoring some Asian refugees. The other people who are involved are nice, but what really changed my outlook was getting to know the refugees themselves. They're terrific! I never really knew someone from another culture before and I've learned that there's an awful lot I don't know. I'm not so smug about our way of life anymore, and I have more respect for others. Besides, they're just great friends.*
>
> (Sixty-three-year-old woman)

Opportunity for personal growth. For much of your life, you may have been too weighed down with responsibility to your family or job to devote much time to developing your skills and interests, to becoming the kind of person you really wanted to be. Much of your effort had to go towards meeting the needs, goals, or wishes of others. It can be much more rewarding to work at achieving your own goals. Most people get a great deal of satisfaction from working to improve themselves. Now you have that opportunity, but it will take some adjustment. Chapter 6 will present some techniques for clarifying your interests, values, and skills, while helping you plan how to use them in ways that are most rewarding to you.

Opportunity for spiritual growth. Most people learn spiritual beliefs and values from their family, church, school, or community as they are growing up. As adults, they either keep this spiritual identity, allow it to lapse, or rebel against it. Regardless of the outcome, they're controlled to some extent by their early learning experiences. Some of your spiritual identity or fulfillment may have come from your job. You'll lose that source, but it opens up an opportunity to find other sources that can be more personally rewarding.

Whether you call it philosophy, religion or just intellectual curiosity, you have the opportunity to really explore your spiritual identity. You can better understand why your values are what they are, what your purpose in life is, and what you need to do to achieve it. You may change some of your beliefs or you may end up feeling more strongly about them than ever before, but either way, they will now be your beliefs instead of something you assimilated from your culture. You'll understand yourself and your world better, and that can be the most exciting and fulfilling opportunity of all.

In addition to taking advantage of these opportunities, the most successful retirees also had two other things in common:

They were open to new ideas. They tended to listen uncritically, to look for positive learning. As you read how others have found solutions, look for something you can use. If you don't like the way they solved a particular problem, forget it. Look for knowledge, not for error. Being too critical can block the way to new learning.

They kept their sense of humor. The ability to see the absurdity in some of your mistakes makes them easier to accept and helps you find the right answer. Notice the similarity in the words *humor, humiliation, humility* and *human* . That's because they all relate to each other. They stem from the Latin word *humus,* which means earth. People with a sense of humor are down to earth. They don't have phony pretensions.

Humor means that something deserves laughter. If someone laughs at your mistakes, that can be humiliating. But if you have humility, you can laugh at yourself and can't be humiliated. And human? Well, Mark Twain once said that humans are the only animals that have the ability to laugh at themselves. And the only ones that have good reason to.

Anticipate Dangers

> *I thought I was going to do just great in retirement. I had thought it through and had lots of plans, things that seemed to have worked for others. But I kept getting more and more depressed. I woke up one morning and realized that it was eight months since I left work, and I hadn't done a darn thing I had set out to do.*
>
> (Sixty-one-year-old man)

No matter how well you've done your personal restructuring, there are some dangers along the road that can block your path to happiness and fulfillment. Since they're the result of changes in your life, they're usually unexpected, things that you thought would never be a problem for you. Here are some dangers you need to be on the lookout for:

Isolation. There's a big difference between solitude and loneliness. If you've spent your career in a job that demanded constant contact with others, you may appreciate some time to yourself. It's especially pleasant if you've made some progress on personal and spiritual growth. But we all need human contact, and you're probably not used to having to seek it out.

Procrastination. You won't have the deadlines to meet that you did when you were on the job. That's a great feeling of freedom, but it also makes it a lot easier to put things off. When you retire, procrastination can mean that you're delaying the enjoyment of the rest of your life.

Imbalance. Productive work, socializing, play, and intellectual and spiritual activity are all important parts of life. You need to find the proper balance of these activities for yourself and then look for ways to include all of them as you go from day to day. Recreation is fine when you first retire. You've earned it. But most people find that after a while they get less enjoyment from pure recreation and feel a need to find productive and intellectually stimulating activities. Without that balance, they get bored and depressed.

Chapter 3, on maintaining structure in a changing life, will have some ideas on how you can prevent isolation, procrastination, and imbalance.

Alcohol and other drugs. There is one danger that is so destructive to the mind, body, and spirit that it deserves special attention, especially since people going through a life transition are at exceptionally high risk. That danger is the abuse of alcohol, prescription drugs, or other mood-changing substances. Most people think that if they've made it to this mid-life stage without a problem, they're safe—but they are not. The risk of substance abuse increases greatly at this time of life. You need to know what the dangers are. In Chapter 8, you'll hear a personal story from someone who fell into this trap without realizing it was happening. It could happen to *you,* but you can protect yourself by understanding how abuse starts and what its warning signs are.

In spite of the changes and the dangers, don't lose sight of the fact that you are going to have more control over your life than you've had in the past. With a better understanding of the changes, opportunities and dangers ahead, you'll be ready to start planning a strategy to achieve the happiness and fulfillment that you deserve.

Start your personal restructuring process by looking more closely at the kinds of changes you can expect, so that you can anticipate and prepare for them. You should also begin to anticipate what kind of opportunities are going to be opened up by these changes in your life. And you need to be on guard against the dangers.

Anticipating Change

To start your planning process:

• List the changes that you think are the most likely to enter your life in the next few years.

• What opportunities and dangers do they present?

Changes	Opportunities	Dangers

Photocopy the "Anticipating Change" list, and put it in a file marked "Personal Inventory." As you read about the experiences of others and examine your own opportunities more closely, you will probably change or add to this list. As you go through the book, come back and do so.

After the chapters on spiritual and personal growth, you should have a clearer idea of what kind of activities and goals you're going to need to make your life rewarding. Your action plan for the future will help you put it all together and develop a plan to get you where you want to go.

Happy Rebirthday!

2

All at Once
I Was Somewhere Else!

Taking Advantage of a Changing World

Visiting a large city for the first time in his life, the man walked into a department store. Fascinated by the opening doors, he stepped into an elevator. Moments later he was found shaking and bewildered on the sixth floor, mumbling something about a "magic room." "What's the matter?" he was asked. "I walked into this little room," he said with awe. "The doors closed behind me. The room shook and rumbled. Then the doors opened, and I was somewhere else!"

Change is sometimes called the only constant in life. Sometimes it's so sudden and unexpected that you're bewildered like the man on the elevator. You might wake up the day after retirement and find that you're "somewhere else!" That kind of sudden change can be a pleasant surprise or bring a disaster. The only thing you can be sure of is that changes are going to happen, whether you're ready for them or not.

There's an old Chinese curse that goes, "May you live in interesting times." It was meant to be a curse because it means that periods of great change can be very difficult. We live in interesting times. There has been more change in our lifetime than any previous generation has ever seen, and the pace of that change becomes faster every day. Still, it doesn't have to be a curse. If you play it right, it can be a blessing. Let's look at some different types of change, and think about how you can make them work for you.

Social Change

> *I think it was easier for Mom. In her lifetime, the role of a woman was pretty well-defined. She had her place in that little town. First she was a mother, then a grandmother, and now she's a nice little old lady that people come to visit and everyone respects. Not that she wouldn't have been a lot better off in today's world. With her brains, she could have had quite a life. It probably would have been more exciting, but she would have had a harder time trying to figure out what to do with her life at each stage. In her day it was all cut out for her. There weren't very many decisions to make.*
>
> (Sixty-seven-year-old woman)

Society changes, and that has a big impact on how you are viewed or treated by others and how you view yourself as your own life changes. Your perspective will affect how you feel about aging, too. You might think about it with fear, indifference or even anticipation, depending on how you have seen others age.

I once had a friend who was very uncomfortable when he was around anyone much older than sixty. He would get restless, angry, almost frantic after awhile. It wasn't like him, and for a long time I couldn't understand it. He finally confessed to me that in the mining community in which he was raised, most of the older people he knew were in poor health or weren't treated well by the community. Even his own parents had always spoken of them with some ridicule. He was terrified at the thought of growing old himself. That's why he was so uncomfortable around older people.

Once he started talking about his feelings, though, he realized that his fears were unreasonable, and he started to develop a more positive outlook. I was fortunate, having watched my own parents age with dignity and good health. They were able to do things for themselves in their later years that were impossible when they were burdened with family responsibilities. I told him how Dad had turned his hobby of woodworking into a second career, and how Mom found enjoyment in volunteer work. They were able to travel, something they'd never had either the time or the money to do. Sharing these experiences with my friend gave him a different perspective. If you've had a negative experience as he did, it might be a good idea to talk about it with someone. It might change your perspective.

The society that you live in creates certain expectations about what you should be doing at each stage of your life. You're expected to be educating yourself at one stage, beginning a career at another, advancing on the job at a certain rate, and retiring at a certain age. As Solomon said, "For everything there is a season." Another philosopher said, "At twenty, the will reigns, at thirty, the wit. At forty, judgment; and after that, character." He was describing how his society expected people to behave at each stage of life.

How you behave or what you do at each stage, and how well you fit in with your society's expectations will have an effect on how your society treats you. This in turn can affect the way you think about yourself and how you establish your own sense of identity. You can choose to conform or you can choose to be a rebel. You can fight these norms or use them to your advantage. However you choose, you should be aware of your society's expectations and how they're changing.

The way that society has treated older citizens for the last half century or so has been something of an aberration. Throughout history most cultures have held their elders in high esteem, revering them for their knowledge, wisdom, and experience. During the late industrial revolution, however, with its emphasis on physical labor, those who were no longer employed lost status in the community. My friend's experience in the mining town in which he lived was a throwback to those days. But the pendulum is swinging back, and that's good news for you.

Think about how society's view of older citizens has changed just during your lifetime. In the 1930s and 1940s, when a person reached the age where they were no longer employed, they usually stayed with or were taken in by their nuclear family. Few people were in nursing homes. Retirement complexes didn't even exist. Grandpa or good old Aunt Martha lived with the family. Depending on the family's resources and Aunt Martha's personality, that might be either good or bad. Most of the time it was probably neutral. It was just the way things were done.

During the fifties and sixties, the country became more affluent. More generous retirement plans and social security benefits gave retired workers more independence, and it became more common for retired people to live on their own. An industry began to grow to supply this population with housing, goods, and services. Some cities or regions of the country became largely populated by older citizens.

> *I remember the first time I visited St. Petersburg, twenty years ago. It took me a few days to figure out why it seemed so strange. Everybody there was old. Even the people in the shops, the gas stations, everywhere. It wasn't exactly uncomfortable, just strange, kind of like being in a foreign country. I went back last month. Boy, has that place changed! Now everybody there is about my age.*
>
> (Sixty-one-year-old man)

Most people who live in these retirement communities are happy with their choice. Some, however, have discovered that while living in a community where everyone is relatively close in age and interests has a certain comfort, they miss the variety of the communities in which they had lived most of their lives.

As this new phenomenon of older citizens as a special class developed, a feeling also grew among younger Americans that the older population was a burden, drawing on resources that could be better spent elsewhere. It was a generation focused on youth. Advertising and entertainment were both aimed at the younger segment of the population. In the movies and on TV, you were unlikely to see anyone who wasn't young portrayed in a glamorous, or even respectful, fashion. Remember those days? You weren't supposed to trust anyone over thirty.

Through the seventies and eighties, the older population increased greatly in size, visibility, and financial and political influence. As a result, we're living in a relatively good time to be growing older.

Changing values in our society have made leisure activities more acceptable. There are more opportunities and activities available to simply enjoy or improve yourself. Resources for continuing education are boundless. Almost every college or university offers specialized courses to increase your knowledge in areas of individual interest. Elderhostels offer programs that provide opportunities for travel or study with a group that shares your particular interests. All larger cities and most smaller ones have organizations designed to provide educational and other services to older citizens.

In the last decade, there has been a growing recognition of the valuable contributions that older citizens continue to make to society. All told, today's older citizen is widely regarded as healthy, wealthy and wise, and more respected than in recent decades. Your prospects are much better than they would have been if you had reached this stage of life thirty years ago.

You have the opportunity to influence the direction of future social change. Get involved with groups, such as the American Association of Retired Persons, that deal with issues that affect you. Learn about these issues and get involved in political or other activities if you want to change things that need changing.

Technological Change

I remember moving from Iowa to South Dakota by horse and wagon. I saw my first automobile when I was eight, my first airplane when I was fifteen. I was over forty when we got our first telephone. I saw men walk on the moon. Now, I can fly to see my kids on another continent in one-tenth the time it took us to move 100 miles. I can talk with anyone I want to, when I want to. I can watch events all over the world on television, and I can watch my great grandchildren grow by seeing them on video.

(Ninety-one-year-old woman)

This woman has witnessed many times more change in technology than a nineteenth century science fiction writer could have dreamed—and she's taking advantage of it. Technological change can be exciting. More than half the items for sale in a department store today didn't even exist at the end of World War II. If you walk through an electronics store, probably every single item on display didn't exist when you were born.

The information age created by this technological revolution has turned the world into a global village, just what Marshall McLuhan predicted back in the fifties. It's much easier to understand how you are part of a larger world. Confucius said, "I live in a very small house, but my windows look out on a very large world," and radio and television have enlarged those windows a million-fold. As we watch the nightly news, we're able to witness firsthand events that impact on the lives of others anywhere in the world. We know a lot more about the world, and it should help us understand more about others, about ourselves, and about our place in the scheme of things.

The pace of change has implications for you as you move through the stages of your life. You may feel that you have been victimized by the technological revolution, that technology has passed you by and made irrelevant those skills that you worked so hard to develop during your career. On the other hand, these same advances can be exciting, and they can add to the quality of your life. They create new challenges and new opportunities for leisure and learning. They can free your time to do other things that are more rewarding.

Certainly the advances in medical technology have made it likelier that most of us will live longer, healthier, and more productive lives. Communications technology makes it easier to stay in touch with loved ones no matter what the distance. It's easier, faster, and less expensive to travel. Education and entertainment are available at the push of a button.

Take advantage of the technological revolution. Make an adventure out of learning how new developments can make your life more exciting or rewarding. You don't have to become an expert. Most new technology is designed to be user-friendly.

Check out your local community college and see if they have an introductory course in computer use. If you're like me, computer-dumb, you'll find it quite a revelation. It's not quite as scary as you might expect. If I can learn how to use a word processor at my age, you can too. It would have taken me at least five times as long to write this book without one. Even if you never get a home computer, by taking an introductory course, you won't feel quite as left out of the technology revolution as you did before.

Television is often scoffed at as the modern opiate of the people. It is, if you sit around watching the soaps or sports every day, but it can also be a marvelous tool for education. Most cable systems have two or three channels that routinely show programs that are educational in nature. And some systems have a channel dedicated to education, where you can even take high school or college courses for credit. If you don't have cable, public television is available nearly everywhere, and it has many educational programs.

I remember when I was in grade school, we would be treated to an educational movie about four times a year. It was always exciting, such an interesting and easy way to learn. It would hype my interest in the subject for weeks afterward. Today you can find at least ten programs every week that are far superior in quality, interest, and learning potential to those old films—and if you own a VCR, the possibilities are almost endless.

Check with your local cable system to find out if they have a public access channel. These programs provide an opportunity for people like you to broadcast their own programs—news of your church's activities, for example, or group discussions about important issues. Dramatic or musical presentations are also a possibility for you or your group. Who knows, maybe you'll become a star!

Don't be afraid of technological change. Think of it as a wonderful way to expand your horizons. Marvel at the opportunities it presents for education, communication, self-expression, and enjoyment. Be glad you live in "interesting times."

Changing Relationships

Before you start examining your relationships, I'm going to tell you a secret. I really hate to do this, because it may put all the psychology departments of all the colleges in the world out of business. From seven years of formal study of psychology at a leading university, reading hundreds of books, plus twenty-five years of experience in counseling people and training managers, I can put all of the accumulated wisdom about how people behave into one sentence. It will apply to just about everyone you ever encounter, except perhaps for some unfortunates who suffer from truly severe psychiatric disorders. What is this secret? **People will behave like you expect them to behave.**

It's been proven scientifically, it's been the subject of

literature, and it's been proven by successful companies in the workplace.

If you believe, as I do, that all people are striving to be good and to do the right thing, then you'll somehow convey that expectation to them through your attitude, your words, and your actions. In return, they will try to live up to your expectations. If you convey through those same actions, attitudes, and words that you expect them to fail, to cheat or to be selfish, then they'll respond by living down to your expectations.

If you're interested in scientific proof of this simple principle, look up Robert Rosenthal and Lenore Jacobson's *Pygmalian in the Classroom* (Holt, Rinehart & Winston, 1968), a classic study in psychology literature. It shows how kids respond to their teachers' expectations. If you want something a little lighter, read George Bernard Shaw's play, *Pygmalion*. A musical based on this play was later made into the movie *My Fair Lady*. If you haven't seen it, I urge you to do so. The leading player, Henry Higgins, conveyed to Liza Doolittle that he believed she could accomplish whatever she wanted to, and so she did.

Long ago, a man named Wally, a friend and mentor, brought this home to me very personally. I was having a lot of conflict with a colleague, Jack. I felt like we were in competition, and I was sure that he was out to get me. I walked into Wally's office one morning and proceeded to unload my feelings about Jack. Wally sat back and let me rant and rave for quite a while. Then he said, "You know Jack pretty well, don't you?"

"More than I'd like," I said.

"Is he a religious guy?" asked Wally.

"Well, he goes to church."

"Do you think he prays?" asked Wally.

"Probably," I admitted reluctantly.

"I bet he gets up every morning," said Wally, "kneels down next to the bed, and says 'Dear God, please help me to be a real son of a bitch today.' Right?"

Of course he didn't do that. Wally's questions made me realize how absurd it was for me to think that Jack was deliberately setting out to be a bad guy. *I* try to be a good person and do the right thing, don't you? Sure you do. Then isn't it ridiculous to think that someone else is deliberately trying to do the wrong thing? Since Wally's lesson, I've always tried to remember that others are just as well-intentioned as I think I am.

It's been hard to keep that positive attitude sometimes, and there have been a few instances when I've been disappointed. I can tell you with assurance, however, that if you believe in the good intentions of others and in the essential goodness of all people, you'll convey that attitude and people will live up to your expectations.

For a variety of reasons, your relationships with others are going to change after retirement, more than they have in the past. Not all of these relationship changes will happen to you, but at least some of them will.

For many people, co-workers are an important part of social life. This usually changes in retirement. You're going to be involved in different activities, and you'll have more opportunities to make new friendships. There may not be as much time left over for maintaining some of your old contacts. As your friends change their lives, some are going to move. It's also a sad fact that you will lose more friends and family members to death.

As you age, your relationship with your parents and children will change. After a lifetime of relying on your parents, they now rely on you. At some point, they will no longer be able to take care of themselves. You need to plan for that. And after a lifetime of having your children depend on you, they reach a stage where they are much more independent.

Job Relationships

Let's start with co-workers, since almost everyone has at least some daily contact with others on the job. This contact provides some real variety in your social life because you're more or less forced to be with these people, whether you would choose to or not. Your work brings you together with people of different ages, ethnic backgrounds, and political and religious viewpoints. Without this forced contact, it's easy to fall into a pattern of associating primarily with people who are just like you. That can be comfortable, but it's limiting. And, frankly, it can get pretty boring.

Look at how you interact with your closest friends at work. If you do things on weekends, socialize at night, attend sporting events, or other things that have no connection with work, there's a good chance the relationship will continue in some form after you leave the job, although you probably won't see your friends as often. But if most of your social activity with them is on the job, or consists of stopping for a drink or some other activity right after work, you probably won't see much of each other after you leave. This usually surprises people, because they were truly good friends—but it usually happens. Several clients have told me, in one way or another, "It's amazing how *gone* you are, once you go."

If you want to maintain those work-related friendships, the time to start changing the pattern is now. Most important, if nearly all your socializing is done with people you know from work, start making an effort to find new friends away from the job or you're likely to be lonely in the future.

Look for ways to maintain the diversity in your relationships that is now provided by your job. You'll stay in better contact with the real world if you have friends from different age groups, socio-economic classes, ethnic groups, and interests. You need to find social activities, volunteer opportunities, education programs, or church activities that involve people from these different groups.

When you're on the verge of retirement, it's a good time to settle old scores with bosses, subordinates, or co-workers. The way you settle them can be good for you, and it can be kind of fun, too. If you've had disagreements or rivalries, if you feel that you've been wronged, or if you've held grudges against anyone at work, go to those people and try to make amends. It doesn't make any difference who was wrong. You don't have to win. The point is to put it behind you. Holding resentments will kill your future happiness.

Don't go to someone and say, "Let's make a deal. If you'll admit you were wrong, I'll forgive you." Or anything like that. Instead, say, "I'm really sorry we've had our disagreements. I'm sorry for anything that I did that caused it. I'd like to put that behind us."

If they try to stir up old issues, don't argue. Just repeat the same sentiment. You'll usually be pleasantly surprised at the positive response you get. It's almost impossible for the other person to continue to hold the grudge, and in those rare cases where they do, you'll feel comfortable in the knowledge that you've done your part to try to settle the matter.

It's easier to forgive the mistakes of others than it used to be. By now, I've made them all myself.

(Seventy-four-year-old man)

Parents

If your parents have already passed on, you might feel you can skip this section—read it anyway. It may help you think about the relationship you had with them and help settle some old feelings. It might also help you better understand your relationship with your own children, if you have any. Your kids probably have about the same feelings towards you that you had towards your parents.

I've learned from my counseling experience that people don't become truly adult until they are able to forgive their parents for being human, and they aren't really mature until they can appreciate them.

There are some children who were emotionally or physically abused by their parents. If that happened to you, you should talk to a therapist, if you haven't already done so. Most people, though, were raised by parents who were trying to do their best, as almost everyone does.

You've probably gone through several stages in your feelings towards your parents. When you were little, the common feelings were love, dependence, respect, and maybe a little fear. You thought your parents knew everything, could do anything, and were sometimes mean because they didn't always let you do what you wanted to do. You didn't always understand that they were trying to protect you or help you to learn. There was a feeling of safety in having the rules established by someone else, and you didn't have to think or make choices for yourself. Some people never mature beyond this stage, and throughout their lives they seek situations where others make their decisions, or they distort religion to provide the same surety.

In adolescence, as you struggled to gain your own identity and become independent, there was probably a stage of rebellion against your parents. There may have been a power struggle of sorts, and sometimes you thought your parents were dictating orders just to show you who was boss. Especially in late adolescence, you began to learn more about the world, as your intellect developed. You learned that your parents didn't know everything, and you might have overreacted to this discovery by thinking that they didn't know anything.

Sometime during your late teens or early twenties, as you approached adulthood, you may have had more appreciation of your parents. This comes with the understanding that they probably tried to do the right thing, but that's difficult to fully appreciate until you raise your own kids. And at this stage, in spite of that appreciation, you were likely to take a more critical and analytical look at how your folks performed. The attitude is often, "Well, I know they tried, but they sure could have done it a lot better." This is the stage where we can forgive our parents for being human.

It's usually in your late twenties, later, or never, that you're able to move on to the next stage in your feelings. It seems as though you have to learn from your own experience just how difficult life can be before you can look back and say, "Wow, that must have been tough. Look at what my parents had to give up to raise me. I'm not talking about material things, but giving up the chance to follow their own dreams—things like that."

> *As Dad was dying, I remember thinking about him with a mixture of admiration and criticism. He was so capable, ingenious actually. He could have done just about anything, but all he ever did was work on that road crew. Why didn't he do more with his life? As I watched him die, I understood for the first time how terribly frustrating it must have been for him. He knew he could do all those things, too, but he had seven hungry kids at home, it was the middle of the Great Depression, and he couldn't risk the security of that $60 a month he was making to try anything else.*
>
> *So he stuck with it. It was a moral decision. He was sure of his values, and he stuck to them. But at what a personal sacrifice! And you know*

what? I bet he never regretted the decision to put his family before his personal ambition.

That insight gave me a depth of respect for Dad that I had never had before. I mean, I always respected him, but this was a powerful feeling. I don't have many regrets. I think I was able to let Dad know how much I loved him before he died, and I've always been grateful for that. But I wish that I could have told him how I finally understood what he had given up for us. That made him something really special. That made him a great man in my mind, as great as anyone who has ever lived.

(Fifty-five-year-old man)

If you could reach this level of appreciation for your parents, it would have a profound and positive influence on your relationship with them as they reach old age.

There comes a time when you become a parent to your parents. You go from a stage where you depend on them, to a kind of equality, to a stage where they depend on you. There will come a time when you'll have to make decisions for them and tell them what they need to do. You may have to decide when they're no longer able to care for themselves and need to go to a nursing home, or have home healthcare supervision. If you have the profound respect for your parents that the person quoted above had for his dad, then they'll feel it. That will make it much easier for them to accept decisions from you. They can do it with dignity, because they know and feel that you respect them.

If your parents are still healthy and self-sufficient, now is a good time to start planning for when they are not. You, or they, don't have to make any decisions or commitments now, nor should you push the issue. It's much easier, however, to discuss this sensitive topic when it isn't an emergency, and when various options are still open.

Ask your parents what they want you to do when you have to take more responsibility for their care. Make it light, but show your concern and interest in how they're thinking about it. You'll likely find that they want to talk about it. You're giving them the opportunity to make their wishes known, and they might be dreading just what kind of decisions you would make if they were infirm or disabled.

Don't make any suggestions at this stage; just find out what they would want. Even if they ask your opinion, at this point just stick to learning more about what they want. It will be far less threatening to them and it will make later discussions about the subject easier.

If there are other family members who should be involved in discussing your parents' needs, get together with them and talk about it. Don't try to sit down and decide what's best for Mom and Dad. Instead, try to agree on a plan as to how those decisions will be made when they become necessary, and be sure everyone is aware what Mom and Dad's wishes are.

If your parents are still alive, start your plan for dealing with this issue *now*. Don't delay the process in hopes that it might be something you won't have to deal with. Take my word for it—you will.

You get much of your identity and value system from your parents and, if you have any children, they'll get much of theirs from you. In this sense you are part of a vast continuum stretching many generations into the past and into the future. Understanding your place in that continuum not only fulfills a basic need to be a part of something larger than yourself, it can help you better understand your parents, your children, and yourself. A unique and useful way to add to this understanding is to write a family history.

I've seldom met anyone over forty who doesn't wish that they knew more about their ancestry. When you're young, it may not seem very important, but later in life, more knowledge about where you came from can help you determine where you fit in the scheme of things, and where you want to go.

> *Learning about my family's past has made me think about how what I do might affect future generations. When I was younger, I didn't have much interest in that sort of thing. As far as I was concerned it was ancient history and certainly didn't affect me. But about a year ago, I got Mom talking about the old days and instead of just dwelling on her own childhood, she started telling me stories she remembered hearing from her parents and grandparents. She hadn't done that before, probably because I never showed any interest.*
>
> *There had just been a series about the Civil War on TV, and it had really captured my attention because it explained so much about*

how we, as a nation, have been shaped by our past. As Mom talked, I realized that her grandfather's brother had been killed in that war. All of a sudden, it wasn't ancient history anymore. There was a direct connection, and it gave me a whole different perspective of time. My mother would have known that guy if he had lived to a normal age. And if that war affected how we behave as a nation, those people probably had an effect on how I behave as a person. It made me realize that I might have some influence on future generations. That was a powerful thought to me!

It really stirred my imagination. I thought about how wonderful it would be if my grandparents had kept a written history and I could read in their own words what their life was like. I started pumping Mom for more stories, and I started writing them down. I also talked to some of my older relatives and learned more about how my family immigrated to this country in the 1820s. I can't quite explain the feeling, but I have a much stronger sense of who I am and where I fit in, and that somehow my being here is important. I also developed a much more understanding relationship with Mom in the process.

I know my kids aren't very interested in this stuff now, but someday they'll be glad I wrote about it.

(Fifty-five-year-old woman)

Children

Think about how your relationship with your parents has evolved, and it might help you as your relationship with your grown children changes. If things have been healthy and happy up until now, that will likely continue, especially if you're dealing successfully with the other changes in your life. However, if you don't find replacements for the identity, socializing, and sources of satisfaction you've had from your job, it's easy to fall into the trap of expecting your family to provide them for you. That can put a strain on your family relationships.

> *Sometimes I want to scream at her, "You're their grandmother, not their mother!" When Mom and Dad were working, they were wonderful grandparents. They loved to have the kids over or take them places, they offered advice to me if I asked for it, and they gave the kids presents on their birthdays or the holidays. But now, it's like that every day. Mom is either over here or calling to ask me to bring the kids over. She buys them clothes without talking to me about it. Dad not only tells me how to raise them, but he decides to discipline them himself, and he openly disagrees with me right in front of them.*
>
> *I'm serious—I'm about ready to move to another city just to get away from it. If I try to talk to my parents about it, they guilt me. "We're only trying to help, you know. After all, they are our grandchildren!" Or to get back at me for*

> *criticizing, they get sick so that I have to take*
> *care of them.*
>
> (Forty-year-old woman)

If you have grandchildren, be grandparents, not parents. If you want to spend more time with them, let the parents know that you're available and let them call the shots. Don't guilt them in the process. If it's the other side of the coin, however, and you feel like you're being imposed upon, set the limits of your involvement and stick to them.

Don't buy gifts for grandchildren without discussing it with the parents first. Do be clear on what standards of behavior you expect when they're in your own home, but let the parents handle discipline issues. And *never* contradict the parents in front of the grandkids.

Don't offer your grown children business or personal advice unless they ask for it, and then try to present it as your opinion, instead of what you want them to do. If you let them know through your attitude that you love them and want to be of help when you're needed, they'll take advantage of it. If you come across as knowing more than they do about how they should live their lives, they'll start avoiding you and resist the advice. If you've developed a life of your own, you won't find it necessary to get your self-worth from continuing to control your children.

Too many don'ts? *Do* look forward to a more relaxed, rewarding, and fulfilling relationship with your extended family in retirement. That's the way it usually happens if you're developing and maintaining healthy relationships elsewhere in your life. You'll only run into trouble if you try to impose yourself on others as a way to replace the socialization you previously got from your job.

Partner

> *I visited my parents about a month after Dad retired. As I was sitting in the kitchen visiting with Mom, I noticed Dad going to and from the laundry room. I didn't notice that Mom was doing a slow burn and I said, "What a deal! You've got somebody to do your laundry for you!" Through clenched teeth she said, "Some deal! He's bored, so he wanders around this place trying to find something to do. Even if he does it right, which is seldom, there's nothing left for me. I was perfectly satisfied with my routine, but he keeps interfering. I wish he'd get a job."*

(Forty-five-year-old woman)

A job provided the opportunity for you and your partner to have activities, interests and friends, both as individuals and as a couple. You each had a routine, only part of which you shared. For many people, losing that individuality puts a strain on the relationship. You usually won't hear partners express this, but given a chance to respond anonymously, they do. When I taught preretirement seminars, I'd pass around a questionnaire asking people to rank their worries or concerns as they looked ahead. After financial security and health, the most frequent response was always "too much togetherness." For most partners it's healthy to continue interests and activities that allow you to maintain the individuality that your work life routine provided.

> *Betty had invited Fred to lunch and I ran into them in the cafeteria. "In all the years we've known each other, Fred," I said, "I've never seen you here." Before Fred could respond, Betty spoke up. "I married him for better or for worse," she said, "but not for lunch."*

Unless you plan differently, you're going to have him "for lunch." You need to decide how much togetherness is right for you, and plan what to do about it.

You may have noticed by now that this book addresses issues that you, the individual, must confront, rather than talking about how couples should plan for the future. There are several reasons for this. First, family systems differ, and many people don't have a partner or an extended family at this stage of life. There are some issues, such as financial planning or deciding where to live, that you need to work out with your partner, if you have one. But as far as deciding where to best invest your energy to get the most out of your life, that's something you'll first have to work out for yourself.

Second, you can't change others, only yourself. You can't do it for your partner. Encourage your partner to go through this personal restructuring process, too. Then you can work together to help each other achieve your goals. Most important, you can't have healthy relationships with others unless you have some confidence in yourself and where you're going.

Friends

Much of the same advice pertains to your relationships with   friends and neighbors. If you've got some good friendships to rely on, you're lucky. They're probably healthy because they have about the right balance now. So don't try to change the balance. Don't expect those friendships to expand to fill your available time. In some cases they might, as both you and your friends have more leisure time, but too much closeness can put a real strain on the friendship.

> *Bob and Janet were our best friends for over ten years. We did a lot of things and spent lots of time together. Then we went on a six day trip in a motor home. We were together twenty-four hours a day. After about the third day, it seemed like 240 hours a day.*
>
> *We're all easy-going, and there weren't any serious incidents, but by the end of the trip, I thought it just might be great if I never saw them again. Afterwards, it took about a month before we started feeling comfortable with each other. Then we were able to talk about it and everyone ended up laughing. Still, the trip nearly ended our friendship, and we know better than to put ourselves in that situation again.*

(Forty-eight-year-old woman)

Don't expect current friendships to fill up all that extra time you're going to have available. It's more realistic, healthier, and more interesting to develop new relationships. New and different activities, which you'll explore in the chapter on personal growth, will provide some opportunities to do that.

Now that you've seen some changes that have affected others, you have probably been giving thought to more changes that you can expect in the next few years.

• Go back to your "Anticipating Changes" chart at the end of Chapter 1 and change or add to your list.

• Start thinking about ways you can make those changes work for you.

3

Start Rockin' Right Now

Keeping Structure in a Changing Life

Frank had been a laborer with the construc-
tion company all his life. He was about to retire
at the end of the current project. "What are you
going to do when you retire, Frank?" I asked
him. "I'm going back to Kentucky," he said.
"I've earned a rest. The first year, I'm just going
to sit on the porch in my rockin' chair."
"Then what?" I asked.
"Then," he said, "I'll start rockin'."

(Fifty-five-year-old man)

It turned out that Frank lived a full and pleasant life
after his retirement thirty years ago. He enjoyed hunting,
fishing, spending time with his grandchildren, and many of
the things he had always planned to do. While he certainly
had earned a rest, he didn't spend all that much time in his
rocking chair. He had been pulling my leg, of course, and
even at age eighteen I was pretty sure that he was joking.
I'm glad he moved past the rocking stage, because if he had
actually followed through on the plan he described to me,

he probably would have had some trouble.

Everyone believes that they want freedom, but there is a certain comfort in not having to make decisions. If your daily schedule is laid out for you by your job, you don't have to make many decisions about what to do next. Having to make your own decisions can cause anxiety. In his book *Escape From Freedom,* psychologist Erich Fromm describes how people sometimes are willing to give up their freedom and be controlled by a dictator—just to gain the comfort they derive from not having to make decisions!

Throughout your life, most of your activities have been controlled by operating within a certain structure. During your years on the job, you would get up at a certain time, go to work at a certain time, and probably even follow the same route to work every day. When you'd get to work, you'd follow a regular routine. You'd talk to various individuals, return your phone calls, go to coffee or lunch with the same people, at the same places. This routine gave a kind of comfort and predictability to your activities. If stress or surprises interrupted, you could go back to this routine as one way of bringing order and comfort back into your life. Following your routine was like having a road map to guide you through life, but in retirement, the map is gone.

> *When I thought about retirement, I always thought about all the things I would have time to do. I even daydreamed about it, visualizing it in my mind.*
> *Simple stuff. It probably doesn't sound too exciting to most people. I'd go to the library— I've always liked that, but I was usually too tired after work. I'd go to art museums. I know*

that sounds like something people talk about but never do. But I did go to them, at least four or five times a year, and always felt like I couldn't spend enough time. Boy, when I retired I'd have time to do it. I'd spend a half day there, and really take my time. I'd do it every month, take in every new display. And I'd keep in shape. I'd work out every day. I did it pretty regularly when I was on the job, but I had to force myself to do it in the morning before work. Now I could take my time, do it right, and enjoy it.

I'd get up when I felt like it, but probably not much later than I did when I was working. I'd take my time reading the paper, have a light breakfast, then I'd go to the club and work out. I wouldn't rush through it like I used to do. That brings me up to about 10 A.M. Then I'd go back home to work on some of my hobbies, or maybe read something worthwhile to improve myself. After lunch, I'd be off to the library or the art museum for a relaxing, but intellectually stimulating, afternoon. Sure, I knew that I wouldn't take in those two places every day, but I'd do something like that. Then I'd go home for dinner and a relaxing evening.

I'd do something new every day. The pace would be relaxed, but still challenging. I'd be learning new things, meeting new people, and doing some volunteer work. It was really pleasant to think about this new routine. These are the things I've wanted to do all my life, and they'd have some value, too. I was going to get smarter, and I would accomplish some things for the good of the world in the process, with the volunteer work and all.

Well, the first few weeks I settled in like I used to when I took a vacation. I just loafed. That was good for me during my working years, because I always pressed a pretty hard pace. But after the first few weeks, instead of starting to follow the routine I had planned, I found myself settling in even more. I slept later every day, not because I was tired, but because there didn't seem to be any good reason to get up. When I did get up, I'd read the paper from cover to cover, not because of interest, but just out of boredom.

By the time I got around to breakfast, it was too late to think about going to work out, so I'd watch the tube instead. After lunch I'd putter around for awhile. I'd tell myself that to-morrow I was going to get going, but I'd end up watching the tube and dozing off in the afternoon.

Of course, I was getting so much sleep during the day that I couldn't sleep very well at night. I'd find myself wandering around the house in the middle of the night feeling vaguely de-pressed and dissatisfied. Losing sleep at night gave me an excuse to sleep late the next morn-ing. I just couldn't get going. I didn't realize what was happening till one day it hit me that it had been eight months since I left the job,

*and I hadn't done a single thing that I had
planned to do. I was depressed and disoriented
because I was keeping such odd hours.*

(Sixty-one-year-old man)

There is even a physical factor involved in the routine
this man described. You may have heard the term *circadian
rhythm.* The word *circadian* means "about a day." It means
that your body and its various functions have their own
daily routine. Many people refer to themselves as a morning
person or a night person. They mean that at a certain time
of day they are more alert, energetic, and can think and
perform better. They're describing their personal circadian
rhythm.

Part of this rhythm is purely physical. If it's not forced
into a specific routine, the body will adjust to its own most
efficient cycle. If it's forced into a different pattern, it will
gradually adjust to a new schedule, but probably won't
quite achieve peak efficiency. If you've ever traveled to a
place that was several time zones away, you've no doubt
experienced this feeling, usually called "jet lag." After a
couple of days in the new time zone, you'll adjust to
sleeping and eating at the same time as the locals, but you'll
find yourself mentally "spacing out" at certain times during the day. You're just not as efficient as you would be
under your normal schedule.

Moving out of the regular daily routine you've established over the years offers some opportunities and some
dangers, depending on your own particular circadian
rhythm and on your personal need to have order and
routine in your life. It's important that you're aware that
changes in this routine can affect the way you feel and
perform. You need to introduce change gradually.

If you make a sudden shift of more than an hour or two in the times that you eat and sleep, it can disrupt your sleep pattern. This sometimes results in feelings of depression or anxiety. If you're not aware of circadian rhythm, you might mistakenly identify these feelings as coming from emotional, rather than physical, sources. You need to know the source of the problem before you can correct it.

In addition to these physical effects, almost everyone needs a certain amount of routine in their life to stay on an even keel. When you first leave the fixed schedule of your job, it's a good idea to maintain a similar pattern in your life, at least for a while. Get up at the same time, and eat at the same time. Schedule physical and mental activities, even though they may be purely recreational, along a schedule similar to the one that you maintained on your job. Introduce change into this pattern gradually. If it works and you feel rested and alert, try some more change. Maybe the new pattern fits your circadian rhythm better than the old one. If, however, you sometimes find yourself feeling tired, even though you've had plenty of sleep, or if you feel depressed or anxious, go back to your old schedule.

Fortunately, I finally realized that I had to do something to wrench myself out of this. I had to find some way to bring some order and purpose into my life. To get started really took an effort, and I had to force myself. I started to make a schedule, set up a week at a time to do the things I always said I wanted to do. It sounds funny to say that I had to force myself to do enjoyable things, but I did. After a while it became easier, and I gradually settled into a positive routine. It is a routine, but I guess I need that to keep some order in my life.

In the early stages of change, it's a good idea to make a flexible written schedule a week or a month in advance. You won't be tied down to it, of course, as you would be on the job, but it can help maintain some structure and security as your life changes.

As you set a new schedule for yourself, be sure to build in some time for exercise—exercise for the body and exercise for the mind. Any health expert will tell you that you need physical exercise to keep your body in condition, but they usually don't mention that physical exercise will also greatly improve your mental outlook. You will need intellectual stimulation, too. To keep physically fit, you need to exercise your body. To stay mentally sharp, you need to exercise your mind.

I really don't feel much like expending any physical energy when I first get up in the morning. It would be so much easier to just sit around the house sipping coffee and reading the paper. I've learned from experience, though, that I'll feel better all day if I get the old body going first. I tell myself, "Come on, you've got to do this. You know it's good for you." I force myself out the door and start walking, reluctantly, but it's only about three minutes into the walk before I'm feeling wide awake and appreciating the morning. A couple of minutes later my mind is starting to work, thinking about all the things I want to do that day, and looking forward to them. The farther I go, the more creative I get. By the time I'm back at the house, twenty minutes later, I'm raring to go.

On the days I don't exercise, I kind of mope
around all day, physically and mentally tired.
                        (Forty-seven-year-old woman)

There are even physical reasons for the mental changes
that take place when we exercise, biochemical changes that
make you feel both more relaxed and more alert. I'll leave
the explanations to the medical experts, but all you have to
do is try it for a few days to appreciate the positive effects.

There's another way that physical activity can affect
your mental outlook, and that's the way you keep up your
physical appearance. If you look sharp and act sharp, you'll
feel sharp!

I had a job where I had to wear a suit every day,
and I was always careful to look neat and trim.
But I was always more comfortable in what I
called my "grubs," casual clothes like warm-up
suits in the winter and shorts and T-shirts in
the summer. I remember thinking that when I
retired, I'd never have to wear a necktie again.
I didn't for about the first three months I was at
home. There was nothing wrong with that, but
I carried it a little too far. I didn't get a haircut,
I started going days without shaving, and I
wasn't getting any exercise. I started feeling
vaguely depressed, and also a little resentful
that my friends seemed to be acting standoff-
ish. Then one morning I looked in the mirror
and said, "You really look like a slob. You're
shaggy, you're sloppy, and you need a shave."
I went for a long walk, came back, and shaved
and showered. I got dressed up for the first time
in weeks, and went and got a haircut. I felt

*better than I had in a long time. Then I called
a friend and took her to lunch at a nice restaurant. She said that I looked like I was on top of
the world, and I felt like it. I still like my grubs,
but I know that I have to take care of myself
physically, that my self-image is affected by
how I do that.*

(Fifty-eight-year-old man)

Keeping Track of Your Life

Another way of keeping some order in your life as you
adapt to your new freedom is to keep a journal. In fact, it's
a good idea to start doing that now, not just after you've
retired. It's a way of checking up on yourself. You can look
back over weeks, months, or years and examine the patterns in your life. Are you headed in the right direction? Are
you making progress towards your goals, or are you just
drifting from day to day? It's a way to keep in touch with
your past while giving direction to your future. Make at
least a few notes every day and review your journal every
week or so. Write about your feelings, not just about events
or activities. You'll be surprised at what it tells you.

*When I read my journal, it's like I'm reading
about someone I used to know, not myself.
That's because the person I used to be isn't the
person that I am now. I'm changing, and most
of the time I'm growing. I want to know about
that other person, though. It helps me understand who I am now.*

*There's another advantage to journaling. When
I just remember events, I think about things I
did or things that happened. When I read my*

*journal, all the feelings come flooding back.
Sometimes I can understand things better than
I did when they happened.*

(Fifty-year-old woman)

Links from the Past to the Future

Rituals can also be an effective way of maintaining some emotional stability over time as your activities and relationships change. They are ways of connecting to your past while allowing growth for the future, a connection between who you were and what you are becoming.

*I went through a period where I thought the
old family rituals around Christmas were pretty
silly and childish, and when we raised our own
family we did things differently. In doing that,
however, we started our own family rituals.
They're different from the ones I grew up with,
but they're still rituals. They meant a lot to me,
but I didn't think they were all that important
to the kids.*

*Last Christmas, I sat up with my twenty-year-
old daughter after everyone else had gone to
bed. She told me she had almost stayed at
college to be with her boyfriend, but decided at
the last minute that she would just feel empty
if she wasn't home for Christmas. She started
to reminisce and dredged up stories from past
holidays. She talked about the special feeling
of warmth and love and belonging. Pretty soon
we were both close to tears, happy ones.*

I started talking about my childhood holidays,

and how we did things then. For two hours we relived those days, both hers and mine. It brought back those feelings of almost perfect love between a little child and a parent, and it brought back the feelings of love I had for my parents, too. She said she was surprised that I had never talked about it before. By the time we were through, we were making plans for next year, including some of the old rituals from my childhood. "Your childhood is part of me, too," she said, "and I'm going to pass everything on to my kids someday." I never felt so close to her as I did that night.

(Fifty-eight-year-old man)

There are rituals in your work, family, social, and spiritual lives even though you don't always call them that. You'll lose your work life rituals when you retire, and those in your family or social life will be affected by changing relationships. You should give some thought to which rituals you want to keep, and how you can go about keeping them.

I still play bridge once a month with three of my high school friends. We've been doing it for forty years, ever since our fifth class reunion. We always play on the first Wednesday of the month, and I bet we haven't missed a dozen times in all those years. I guess you could call it a ritual. We've changed a lot, and we don't have much in common other than our school days, but it's really important to me. I kind of go back in time and become the girl I was then, and it helps me understand the person that I

*am now. I really enjoy those games, and I think
it's good for me.*

(Fifty-eight-year-old woman)

Class reunions, Saturday golf, or attendance at concerts or sporting events are all examples of social ritual. They provide a foundation of social stability upon which you can build new relationships and adventures.

One of the many benefits of religious affiliation or church attendance is the ritual involved. In Chapter 4, you'll recall some of the ways this contributed to how you became the person you are. You can examine some ways to use these old rituals in your spiritual growth.

*About ten years ago I stumbled across this little
church in a town about forty miles from here.
It looked almost like the one I went to as a child.
I attended a service, just out of curiosity, and
darned if the service wasn't even similar to
those I attended when I was just a kid, kind of
old-fashioned. I started going over there four
or five times a year. It's not so much the
memories that it brings back, it's the feelings.
Feelings of contentment, hope, and security
that I had when I was a kid.*

*A few times over the years when I was having a
bad time or feeling kind of lost, I've gone over
there and sat in the empty church, just thinking. It didn't seem like praying, but I suppose
you could call it that. After awhile, I'd start
feeling peaceful and centered, like I knew where
I was going. And I'd have some faith that
everything would turn out all right.*

(Fifty-five-year-old man)

Examine your rituals and think about the ways they contribute to your stability and feelings of well-being. You may want to eliminate some, but think it through. They probably wouldn't have become rituals if they weren't filling an important need for you. You'll want to strengthen other rituals to maintain continuity in those areas of your life that are undergoing the most change. Look back on the rituals from your youth that have fallen by the wayside over the years, and think about whether you want to reintroduce them into your life. Those that involve church or family may be a pleasant way to strengthen your connections to your past and future.

You might decide to develop some new rituals to aid in your stability and growth. If there are some activities that are important to you, but that seem to get pushed aside too often, you might want to look for ways to ritualize them, especially if they involve others. Set aside a certain time, like the third Wednesday of every month, to get together with friends and do those activities.

It will take both creativity and discipline to make positive changes in your life's structure. You should make use of the freedom that you will have to try new adventures and open up new possibilities for yourself. Be an adventurer, and seek out new challenges. Don't be afraid to fail. At the same time, keep some discipline in your life. Maintain a structure within which to explore your new freedom, at least until you're comfortable with a new routine.

If you've already got some systems in place to keep tabs on yourself (such as a schedule or a journal) and some steadying influences in your life (such as ritual), then now, before you retire, is the perfect time to start experimenting for the future. Try to break out of your regular routine and see how it feels. Alter your hours on the job, if that's possible. Reverse your Saturday and Sunday afternoon schedules. Leave earlier or later for work, and try a totally different route. Eat breakfast at a restaurant instead of at home. Try some new activities. Experimenting with your routine will be a way to learn how easily you adapt to change in the structure of your life.

Rituals

• What are some rituals that will help you maintain continuity in your life?

• Photocopy this chart, and keep it in your "Personal Inventory" file.

Religious

Family

Cultural

Friends

Personal

Other

4

How Did I Get Here?
Why Am I Here?

I never gave much thought to spirituality. It sounded kind of pretentious to me. I always considered myself a religious person, and that took care of it, until the sudden changes in my life made me take a different kind of look at myself. I began to realize that I did have spiritual values, things that affected the way I thought and acted, and I didn't get them all from my church attendance. I wanted to know more about that part of me.

(Fifty-one-year-old woman)

Spirituality is the search for meaning in your life. It examines such questions as:

"Why am I here?"

"Why do I exist?"

"What is the purpose of my life?"

"How did I get to be like I am?"

"Am I what I should be, or should I be trying to change?"

"How do I know what is right and what is wrong?"

"Where do I fit in the universe?"

"Where do I fit in the flow of time—those who came before me and those who will come after? What did they prepare for me and what can, or should, I leave for future generations?"

The answers to these questions will help define your spiritual identity. What you truly want to be, try to be, is in some way what you are. Your aspirations, your hopes, represent your values, and values are an important part of what you are. If you are clear on what your values are, they will give you more control over the direction of your life. Values will provide a framework within which to judge for yourself the morality or goodness of your decisions and your actions. They will be the foundation on which to build your future spiritual growth.

You probably never thought of it this way, but your job or your career may have given you some opportunities to express or even fulfill some spiritual values and goals. Your work may have provided a focus for your purpose, or a way of participating and belonging, for example. The feedback you got from others was one way of validating the right or wrong of your actions. Some of that fulfillment that you now get from work is going to change, and it might leave you feeling a little empty. The change can also be an opportunity to work towards your spiritual goals in ways that can be even more satisfying.

This chapter is not about "religion." Religion is a way you choose to express, reinforce, share, or practice your beliefs and your values. It can be a way for you to profess your faith to the rest of the world. It can also be a way for you to fill a basic spiritual need, the need to be part of something greater, to belong.

For some, identification as a member of a church or a particular religion is a way of convincing themselves that they're being spiritual, when they may not actually be examining their values and holding themselves account-able for living up to them. Billy Sunday once said, "Going to church doesn't make you a Christian, any more than going to a garage makes you an automobile." The same could be said for the mosque, the temple, or any other place of worship. Spirituality comes first. Know what you believe, then use your religion to practice and dem-onstrate those beliefs.

There seems to be a spiritual hunger in every human being. Some are never able to fill that hunger, or even feed it. Others go through life making progress towards fulfill-ment, but they feel a vague discomfort that they aren't doing the "right thing." It's not just a matter of having spirituality or not having it. The basic hunger for these feelings is so overwhelming that if it isn't fed by healthy spirituality, you're likely to pursue unhealthy ways to try to satisfy it. Those who are content are those who are some-how nourishing their spiritual needs through what they do or what they are. Those who aren't content, often franti-cally strive to feed the hunger through means which are not fulfilling.

There is a fascination today with addictions. Many, possibly all, of the behaviors labeled "addiction" are actu-ally unhealthy ways that people are using to try to find spiritual fulfillment. To label these unhealthy attempts to find fulfillment "addictions" may be accurate, but it focuses on the wrong aspect of the behaviors. It doesn't identify the needs that people are trying to satisfy, so there isn't any way to develop a plan to satisfy those needs in better ways. As you examine your spiritual life, you should first try to identify the spiritual hunger, ask yourself whether you are pursuing unhealthy means to try to feed it, and look for ways that are healthy and fulfilling.

Some people are able to find true spiritual fulfillment. Many who have done so have told me that it only happened in later life and for many, after they had retired from their primary career. Why so late?

For some, it takes a dramatic upheaval in their lives to cause them to examine their values. Others don't realize what an integral part of life spirituality is until time and experience gives them better insight into the meaning of life. They are too caught up in themselves or in a frantic effort to prove something to the rest of the world. Substitutes like material or social success work for a while. They don't have, or don't take, time to examine themselves and their lives. They're working to please or impress others.

With age comes understanding; with retirement comes freedom from restrictions. For some, that understanding and freedom opens the door to the most fulfilling adventure of their lives.

> *I've done reasonably well, and I've had a satis-*
> *fying life. I think I did a good job raising my*
> *family, I had some religion in my life, I went to*
> *church and all. I'm not ashamed of it, but when*
> *I look back now, there was always a vague*
> *feeling that there could be more, or that some-*
> *thing was missing. After I retired, a lot of my*
> *reference points were gone. The job was gone,*
> *and the kids didn't need me anymore. I was*
> *forced to deal with me—who I was, and what I*

stood for. At first it was a little disconcerting,
but I had a good talk with a friend who had
gone through the same thing. She said, "Well,
why don't you figure out who you are and what
you stand for? You might like what you find!"
She made it sound like an opportunity instead
of a problem.
So I did figure it out, and I'm not too disappointed in what I found. It also helped me
realize that there's a lot more that I can know
about myself, and there are some things I'd like
to change. Some things I am changing. I'm
finding that there's more to life—some of that
stuff I thought was missing. I'm not perfect and
I never will be, but I'm making progress. My
minister told me, "You won't attain perfection.
You're neither Christ nor Buddha. But if you're
making progress, that's more than many people
ever achieve."

(Sixty-one-year-old man)

Spiritual Growth

Some call it religion, others call it intellectual curiosity
or philosophy. Under any name, it is an exciting and
profoundly fulfilling pursuit. You probably never thought
of yourself as a *philosopher*. It sounds pretentious, but you
probably are one. The name comes from two Greek words
that mean *one who loves knowledge.*

I don't recall ever meeting anyone who didn't like to
learn something new. If you weren't seeking new knowledge, you wouldn't be reading this book. So, for the purposes of this exercise, at least, call yourself a philosopher.

It will give you the right attitude.

Speaking of attitudes, take a look at how one person learned to have an open mind:

> *When I was in my twenties, I went through a period when I thought I was a real intellectual. You have to be young to be dumb enough to think you know everything. I read an enormous number of books, some heavy stuff, and I even understood some of it. I loved to get into arguments about philosophical issues, and I especially loved to try to prove that the other person's beliefs were wrong.*
>
> *Fortunately, I had a mentor, a man much older and wiser than I was. Also, fortunately, I had enough respect for him that when he talked, I listened. One day we went together to hear a lecture on spirituality. After the lecture, Wally asked me what I thought of it. "Well," I said in my usual condescending fashion, "he was a very good speaker, but he sure was wrong about—and I proceeded to describe all of his points that I thought were wrong. Don't you agree?"*
>
> *"Gosh," Wally said. "I didn't pay any attention to all the things I couldn't agree with. I was listening for things I could agree with, or learn something from." When he saw that he had hit home, he proceeded to give me one of his rare lectures.*
>
> *"You know," he said, "you spend all that time and brain power reading and studying, but you're always looking for something that you*

*can argue against or try to disprove. You're
going to end up with a tremendous store of
ideas you don't agree with. I just don't see
how you're ever going to find any of that
very useful.*

*"Now, if you'd just look and listen for some-
thing that you can agree with, something useful, think where you'd be. The speaker may
spend two hours talking about things you don't
like, but if you learned one thing that you
hadn't known before, you'd come away a richer
man. Instead, you wasted the whole evening."*

(Fifty-two-year-old man)

If you can keep this attitude, to try to find what you can learn from other people, from other faiths and from other cultures, you too will come away a richer person. Don't waste your time looking for error. Look for knowledge instead. Be like the anonymous poet who said he belonged to "the great church that claims the good in every race and clime; that finds with joy the grain of gold in every creed, and floods with light and love the bit of good in every soul." Search for the grain of gold in every creed, and the bit of good in every soul.

And search for the bit of good in your own soul. My counseling experience has taught me that there is a spiritual hunger in every human. You may not have recognized or defined it as such, but it's there, and it's something good about you. It's a longing for a connection to a larger purpose than pure physical existence; it's a longing for a feeling of peace and fulfillment, a need to give and receive love, a longing to be wanted, needed, and to feel important or recognized, and a desire to be a good person. It drives you to try to be the best person that you can be.

These seem to be some universal longings that nearly everyone tries to fill:

• To love and be loved.

• To be a part of something greater than yourself. To "belong" somewhere. To have a feeling of "oneness" with your universe.

• To be immortal. Or at least to leave a legacy behind, some mark that you have been here.

• To be good—to meet your own standards of right or wrong.

• To embrace a purpose for living, and feeling that there is a reason for your existence. To feel you are in the right place at the right time, doing what you were meant to do.

• To accomplish something that makes the world a better place.

How you have been striving to feed your spiritual hunger defines your spiritual identity. As you move into this major life change, this is a good time to be sure that you know yourself. Decide whether you're the person you want to be, and choose where you want to go in the future.

Spiritual Identity

Your values and beliefs, your moral standards, and your spirituality are surely the most important factors in making you who you are. Historically, few people have had the luxury of being able to really examine those facets of themselves. Too caught up in day-to-day survival and responsibility, it is easier to fall back on deeply ingrained early learning than it is to engage in self-scrutiny.

A Confucian scholar, Mencius, said, "He who knows his essential nature, knows heaven." Maybe you think you've already examined your life well, that you know your beliefs, your moral standards, and your values—and maybe you do. You can still gain from examining your life a little more closely. You'll not only understand yourself better, you'll find out how other people reach their value systems. It will help you understand and appreciate the beliefs of other people and other cultures. Life will be more interesting, and you might even learn something. Even if you don't, maybe you'll at least rearrange some of your prejudices.

Most people first establish their spiritual identity from what they learn as children. They adopt the beliefs of their parents, of their church, or the community and culture in which they live. As they become adults, they either keep these values or rebel against them. Either way, they're still controlled by a system of belief that they did not choose for themselves.

> *Almost every day I have a debate inside my head. Should I do this the American way or the Chinese way? I've been here ten years, and most of the time I feel like the American way would be what I want and what would be the best for me. But almost every time the Chinese part of me wins the debate.*
>
> (Thirty-seven-year-old woman)

Those values you carried over from childhood have a powerful emotional effect on you, even though rationally you might believe differently. You shouldn't automatically reject that early learning; it can have a great deal of value. You should, however, try to distinguish what's emotional and what's rational. What is a carryover from what you were taught, and what is a belief that you have developed from your own experience?

To reexamine your beliefs is not to suggest that you need to change them, nor does it question the concept of faith. If you're confident that you're on the right path, it shouldn't be threatening to examine what you believe. You'll probably end up more confident than before, and there will be some payoffs. Your values will now be yours instead of your parents' or your culture's. You'll appreciate your beliefs more, and it will be more rewarding to live up to them as a result. It will be easier to make moral decisions because you'll be clear about your standards.

Before you can go on to spiritual growth, you need to understand what your spiritual identity is right now. Be honest with yourself about what you believe in, what you believe your purpose in life is, and what your moral standards are. On what do you base your judgments of what is right and what is wrong? What are you striving for, and how does that fit in with your belief system?

Be honest; no one is going to hear the answers to those questions except yourself. You don't have to be judgmental or condemn yourself for not having the kind of spiritual identity you think you should have. You can't do much about the past, but by doing something in the present, you can do a great deal about the future.

A good way to start your spiritual growth odyssey is to try to better understand how you became the way you are. Where did your beliefs and values come from? What were your earliest experiences that instilled in you a feeling of love or of purpose, of being part of something larger than yourself? What were your first experiences of feeling that something you did was either right or wrong? How did that early learning affect the ways you have tried to feed your spiritual hunger?

Love

One of the most universal spiritual longings is the need to love and be loved. It contributes to the satisfaction of other spiritual needs like peace, contentment, or belonging. Your early experiences with this feeling affect the way you understand this need in later life, and how you seek to fulfill it.

It's the earliest memory that I have. I was probably only three, maybe even younger. My dad would sit in a rocking chair after supper and listen to the news on the radio. In those days, we looked at the radio while we listened, like you look at the tube now. Dad would pick me up and put me on his lap. I would settle back into the crook of his arm and I would feel safe and warm and loved. I felt close—close to my beginning. After all, I was part of him.

Being part of something—that's part of the feeling. It must be what real Christians mean when they talk about being part of the mystical body of Christ. I never wanted to leave that spot—ever. I felt peace and contentment. I had it—the total feeling. Maybe that's why I search for it now. I wonder if someone who never felt it tries so hard to find it, too.

(Fifty-eight-year-old woman)

This person's reminiscence touches on many aspects of spirituality: our search for peace and contentment, how we feel love, and how we give love to others. It's how we seek the security of being part of something greater than ourselves as a way to feel love, peace, and contentment.

Why did that love feel so perfect? I've thought

*a lot about it lately. It was just there. It didn't
demand anything, didn't expect anything. It's
the closest you can come, I think, to understanding the love of God. I realize now that I've
gone through life looking for that feeling again.
I've come close, but never quite gotten there.*

Try to remember the earliest time you felt loved, or felt
love for someone. Relax and close your eyes, and try to
recapture the feeling. For a while, at least, don't try to
analyze it, just feel it. Be prepared, it might be bittersweet.
There may be both beauty and pain in the memory.

*I am overcome by the beauty of the memory.
But why do I feel pain and sadness, too, when
it's the beauty that overwhelms me? Maybe
you can't feel the beauty unless you feel the
pain. I want to share it. Could I? It would have
to be with someone I love. Or maybe I would
love anyone who could share it. Is this how, or
why, we love?*

The pain probably comes from the feeling that you can
never quite recreate that experience, or its perfection. The
search for that perfect feeling of love is the basis of all
religions. Rabbi Hillel, when asked to condense the message of the scriptures to one sentence, said, "You shall love
your neighbor as yourself. All else is commentary."

*You know what I've discovered at this stage of
my life? It's easier to give an undemanding
kind of love than to receive it! I can't make
anybody love me like that, but I can love them.
That's under my control. Of course, there's
a bonus. When I do that, I get a lot of love
in return.*

Forgiveness

In order to give and receive unconditional love, you need to remove any obstacles that stand in the way. Resentment blocks your ability to give love, and guilt can make it difficult or impossible to receive it. So you've got to learn to forgive both yourself and others.

> *I've always been hard on myself when I think I haven't lived up to what I should be. Sometimes it was hard for me to believe that I deserved to be loved. A few years ago, when I was trying to get my life in order, I learned a lesson that really changed all that. I had joined a Bible study group, and we were discussing the story of the prodigal son. Of course I knew that story, but with the struggle I was going through at that time, it was especially meaningful. I made some remark about how consoling it was to think that the father accepted the son back into his household. "I think you missed the point," said Ed, the group leader. "He didn't just accept him back. He came out of the house and went down the road to meet him. He showed that he wanted him back. He forgave him."*
> *Somehow that really hit home. For the first time in my life, I felt like I could not only be forgiven for my shortcomings, but that I could forgive myself. It made me feel OK about myself, worthy of the love of others.*
>
> (Fifty-two-year-old man)

Forgive yourself. Stop blaming yourself for faults in your past (that doesn't mean denying responsibility for them). If there's anything you can do to make up for them, do it. Then get on with your life. Spend your energy on something you *can* do, which is to try to live your life better in the present. The only real fault you can be guilty of is not trying to change your faults.

Now apply those same standards to the way you treat others. Look at the word *forgive*. A big part of it is *give*. Forgiveness is something that you give to others, not something that they have to earn. Holding resentments or grudges, judging or blaming others, will keep you from giving and receiving love.

> *I had some things happen to me in my career that didn't seem very fair. They even seemed downright hurtful at the time. If I had carried resentment about that into retirement I'd still be moping about it and I'd be feeling sorry for myself. I knew I couldn't do that and be happy. I talked it over with an old friend who's given me good advice before. He talked about his belief in people, and that everyone usually tries to do the right thing. He said that when people do something hurtful to others, it's usually out of fear or cowardice. I could believe that, and it meant that they probably had been hurt more by what happened than I was. That realization was a release—a freeing up. I was able to go back to those people and just try to be friends again. The resentment's gone.*

(Sixty-year-old woman)

When you're free of guilt and resentment it's easy to receive love, and it makes it easy for others to give it. If you make no demands and set no conditions on the love you give to others, you won't be disappointed. The giving is reward enough.

Morality

Then there was right and wrong. You knew
which was which. If Mom and Dad approved, it
was right. If they didn't, it was wrong. Simple.
We might not agree with their view, but it was
still wrong, and we knew it. We learned guilt
real early. There was safety in that, though,
because we didn't have to deal with ambiguity
or do a lot of thinking about it—or question
our own thinking.

(Sixty-year-old man)

There's a feeling of security in following moral standards set by someone else, by your parents or by your culture. You don't have to think or take responsibility for your actions. There may be times, however, when you're not sure of your decisions and you have the vague feeling that you're not doing the right thing, even though you're doing what you were taught. When you feel that way, it's often because you're basing your values on what you were told, rather than what you deeply believe yourself.

I remember Father Woerdehoff. He was every-
thing an authoritarian society needed. He was
a big man with a deep, loud voice, confident in
his moral authority. Everyone, adults included,
feared his judgment like they feared the wrath
of God. Actually, in fearing the wrath of God,
they feared Father Woerdehoff, because there
was serious confusion in everyone's mind, es-
pecially my own, as to where God ended and

Father Woerdehoff began.

In later years, I came to appreciate him. I suspect he never had any doubts about his role, though he probably had some about his wor- thiness. I'm sure he felt he was a pastor with total responsibility for his flock and we, by God, were his sheep. If any one of us strayed, it was gonna be his ass with God. So he took personal responsibility to see that none of us strayed. The responsibility must have been awesome. I learned a lot from him.

I never knew, though, who was God: my father, who was always right; Father Woerdehoff, who decided whether my father was right; or God, who was pretty remote. I finally decided on Father Woerdehoff, because he looked and acted the most like God.

(Fifty-five-year-old man)

Where does your sense of right and wrong come from? Is it from the *Bible,* the *Torah,* or the *Koran?* From parents, community, or culture? Some believe that the sacred scriptures are the word of God; others believe that they reflect the accumulated wisdom of society through the ages, or both. Often, though, people believe they are basing morality on the scriptures, when in reality they're basing it on parents, community, or culture. On what they were told the sacred writings teach, rather than what they actually say.

Be sure you *know* what you think you know, and that your beliefs are yours. Lao Tzu said, "It is a noble learning to realize that our knowledge is ignorance." Mark Twain said, "It ain't what people don't know that gets them in trouble, it's what they know that ain't so."

Not Having Yet Made Myself Perfect...

Some people try to achieve a feeling of morality by adopting a rigid code of standards that will provide an easy answer to every situation, without the need to think about it. That can be good, if you are sure of your standards and they are truly yours. But others use this same method to reassure themselves of their moral superiority by applying their standards to others and comparing themselves favorably. You can't possibly understand the reasons behind the behavior of others, so there is no way you can judge them fairly. Confucius said, "As for me, not having yet made myself perfect, I have no time to judge others." Neither do you.

Boy, I must have been obnoxious. I thought I had a monopoly on morality, and I judged everybody else's behavior. I always let them know the verdict, too. I was a Christian, see, and in my mind one of the only real ones around. If someone didn't agree with me or do things my way, it was because they were a sinner. So I felt especially superior to anyone who didn't agree with me. It was easy to feel morally superior and sure of myself.

I don't think anyone from my own crowd ever could have gotten through to me, but I had a co-worker from India, a Hindu. He was always gentle and courteous to me, so I assumed he was as impressed with me as I was with myself. One night we were sitting in his office and I was criticizing the behavior of a mutual acquain-

tance. "You know, I've been reading your Bible,"
he said, reaching in his desk and pulling out
the New Testament. I was amazed and pleased,
thinking that my good example was convert-
ing him to Christianity. "And I think I've found
you in here," he continued.

Certain that in his ignorance he was misunder-
standing the gospel, I asked him what he meant.
He thumbed through for a while and then said,
"Ah! Here you are. The Pharisee standing in
the temple saying 'I thank thee, God, that I am
not like the rest of men.'" Before I could re-
cover, he chuckled and said, "You know, I
believe that you are really a good man, but who
gave you the right to judge others? Even your
own scriptures say 'judge not, that ye be
not judged.'"

Not only did he destroy my wall of phony
superiority, but he became a close friend and
even a mentor. After I got over my hurt feel-
ings, we started having some serious discus-
sions about religion and morality. He knew far
more about other religions and cultures than I
did, and he was able to show me in a non-
threatening way that all people are striving for
moral behavior, and that none of us has a
lock on it.

Later on, I asked him how he had ever been able
to put up with me. He replied, "Ghandi taught
us that we should even be tolerant of intoler-
ance." That got me interested in Ghandi, and I
ended up taking a course on comparative reli-

*gions. I haven't changed my own, but I under-
stand it much better than I did before. I'm a lot
more tolerant of others, and less judgmental,
at least I hope so. Now I know why I had to act
as if I was sure about what was right for
everyone else. It was because I wasn't really
confident about what was right for me.*

(Sixty-three-year-old man)

When you're confident about your own standards, you don't find it necessary to feel superior as a way of reassuring yourself that you're right. In order to gain that confidence, you need to understand where your standards came from and how you adopted them. Give some thought to why you believe what you do about right and wrong. Read or study about the ethics of religions and cultures other than your own. Better yet, have some open discussions with people from your own faith, and with some who have a different background. You'll understand your own beliefs better and have more respect for others.

If you examine your moral standards, they may very well end up being the same as those you were taught, but you'll have more confidence in them because they're yours.

*Throughout most of my life, if you had asked
me on what I based my judgments of right or
wrong, I would have said it was on the Judeo-
Christian tradition. I believed that myself. But
now I realize it was more often a reaction to
what my dad or Father Woerdehoff told me was
right. Even today, when people chide me for
being a slow eater (I'm always careful to clean
up the very last crumb on my plate), I'm only
half joking when I say, "I have to clean my*

*plate, or Dad might come down from heaven
and punish me."*

*I believe that most of what they taught me is
right. The problem is that I followed those
precepts out of fear of punishment. They weren't
my precepts. Now, through study and self-
examination, I think I know why I believe what
I believe. It's not much different than what I
was taught. I don't think Dad or Father
Woerdehoff would disapprove. But it's mine.
Now I can act out of conviction instead of from
fear. It's easier, it's more rewarding, and it
makes me feel good about myself when I believe I'm doing the right thing.*

Courage

Understanding how you developed your moral standards will help you be clear as to what your principles are,
and that should make it easier for you to decide when you
have to take a moral stand. Taking that stand, however,
sometimes demands real courage. Confucius said, "The
inferior person talks about principles. The superior person
demonstrates them by action."

*"I'm just not going to do that. It's against
my principles."*

*"If you don't do it, I'm going to clobber you over
the head with this baseball bat!"*

"OK, OK, I'll do it!"

"What made you change your mind?"

"Nobody ever explained it to me so well before."

Do you stand up for what you believe in? Are you willing
to take any personal risk to defend your principles, or do

you back down when someone "explains it well enough?"
How do you decide where to draw the line, or as the poet
said "whether to fight or run away, and live to fight
another day?"

> *A friend of mine was treated very unfairly at*
> *work, accused of something she did not do. I*
> *wanted to defend her, but I was afraid that if I*
> *did, I might lose my job. I tried to help, but I*
> *didn't have the courage to stand up and say*
> *that if she was terminated, I would leave, too.*
> *I've been ashamed ever since. She's forgiven*
> *me, but I haven't been able yet to forgive*
> *myself. Nothing makes me more miserable*
> *than knowing I didn't have the guts to stand up*
> *for what was right. Cowardice doesn't need to*
> *be punished—it creates its own hell.*

(Forty-two-year-old man)

History is full of examples of people who were willing to
give their lives to defend a principle or a belief. They're
called martyrs. No one can decide for you where to draw
that line, or judge the morality of the decisions you make.
That's always a personal responsibility, but it's one that you
must live with after you've made it. That's easier to do if
you're clear in your own mind as to what principles
guided that decision.

Purpose

A feeling that there is a purpose to your life, a reason for
being, gives meaning and direction to your thoughts,
actions, and morality, and contributes to a feeling that you
are part of a larger purpose for humankind. Your purpose
can be as simple as enjoying the gift of life or trying to

brighten the lives of those around you. It can be as worldly as making a lot of money, as general as making the world a better place, or as specific as believing that there is something in this world that you alone must do. What's important is that you're able to define what you think your purpose is. That will give you the motivation to work towards it, and satisfaction when you achieve your goal.

Your job provides some sense of purpose in your life. It may provide you with goals and a sense of direction, working with others towards a common goal, or a feeling of being needed by others. You'll find it more rewarding, though, to identify and work towards a purpose in life that transcends your job.

As your life changes, as it will with retirement and aging, you may have to find different ways to fulfill your purpose. This woman was quite clear on her purpose in life, so as her circumstances changed, she was able to find new ways to try to fulfill it:

> *I guess I'd have to say that my main purpose was just to try to make life better for the people around me. As I look back, the first time that really meant much was when I was married and raising a family. I did my best for those kids because I wanted them to have a decent life, to grow up to be good people, and to amount to something. It must have been the right choice because I gave up a lot for that, and I've never regretted it. They turned out great, and it makes me feel good now.*
>
> *After the kids were grown and my husband died, for a while my main purpose was just to survive. I had to get a job to pay the rent and*

buy food. There wasn't much available in our little town, but I got a job as a cashier in the local supermarket. It wasn't too much fun at first, but after a while I started enjoying the constant contact with people coming through the store. I did my darnedest not only to be a good cashier, but to be friendly and helpful. I'd feel especially good if I thought I'd cheered up someone who was really down. There's one old grouch who's been a special challenge. I'm determined to make him smile someday, but I haven't succeeded yet. He comes in more often than he used to, though, and he always goes through my line even if the others are shorter! I'll get that old geezer yet.

I'm going on social security in a few months and I'll really miss the store. But I'm planning to start going to the nursing home and visiting people because it's just so darn much fun making them smile.

(Sixty-one-year-old woman)

Many people use their job as a way of working towards their purpose, and this woman did so in an exceptionally meaningful way. If that "old geezer" feels that he's important to someone as a result of her efforts, she has accomplished more towards making life better for others than many people ever do. And she's already planned how she can continue working towards her purpose in life after she retires.

Some who use a job as a way of fulfilling their purpose don't fare so well. Contrast the positive experience of the woman quoted above with the following man who tells how he felt six months after retirement:

> *I gave my all to my job. I didn't think of it in terms of "purpose," but it must have been, because that's where I put all my energy. I measured my success by the bottom line, and focused on cost-cutting and productivity until it was almost a mechanical thing. I didn't pay much attention to how people were feeling, or whether what I was doing had any worth other than showing a profit.*
>
> *The bottom line improved, so I felt I was accomplishing what I was supposed to do in the world. I'm sure I did accomplish something worthwhile and I'm not ashamed of working hard, but I do feel disappointed as I look back. There doesn't seem to be any lasting effect, and I can tell that no one misses me much back at the plant.*

(Sixty-six-year-old man)

This fellow didn't give much thought to how his efforts were contributing to a larger purpose. If he had, he might have accomplished the same things, but in a better way, and with more lasting effects.

That's what happened to this woman, who had a different set of priorities on her job. As a result of the way she tried to fulfill her purpose, she was not only a successful manager, but continues to have a positive effect on the lives of others long after retirement. Here's her story:

> *Early in my career, I had a mentor who took real responsibility to help me develop my career. She did it with others, too. I admired her very much, and I often wondered if the com-*

pany appreciated how she contributed to our success by the way she developed people. I think they probably didn't.

I wanted to be like her, and I consciously tried throughout my career to mentor people the way she did. My greatest rewards came when I'd see one of my protégés move up the ladder, and I could have a secret feeling that I had at least a little bit to do with their success. In our company, though, you don't get much feedback, and I was never sure whether I had accomplished much or not.

I retired a year ago. Last week I got a letter from someone who worked for me a long time ago. Among other things, she said, "You have been one of the most influential people in my life. Even when you were hardest on me, I never doubted your belief in me as a human being, or your respect for me as an individual."

All by itself, that letter makes me feel that I've fulfilled a worthwhile purpose in life. I can feel like I've done something that will last after I'm gone, because that woman is going to help others just like my mentor helped me.

It'll just go on and on.

(Sixty-six-year-old woman)

When I Thought My Life Was Ending, That Was the Only Thing that Mattered

My first exposure to formal religious training was the Baltimore Catechism that the nuns used to teach us in first grade. The first two items were wonderfully concise and all-encompassing:

Q. Who made you?
A. God made me.

Q. Why did God make you?
A. To know Him, to love Him, and to serve Him.

> *Now I happen to believe, sixty years later, that*
> *the answer to the second question is correct.*
> *The problem is, I've been trying to figure out*
> *for sixty years just how I go about doing that.*
> *If I knew the answer, I could tell you what my*
> *purpose in life is.*

(Sixty-seven-year-old man)

One way of getting a clearer picture of what your inner self, your spirit, is telling you about your purpose in life is to think about what you would do if you knew you had only a very short time to live. Some of you may have had a "near death experience." I don't mean the kind where people have cardiac arrest and are pulled back from the brink by a medical miracle, but you may have had a situation where you thought you were going to die, either immediately or in a short period of time. Several people have told me how they felt under those circumstances.

> *I was in a restaurant and had a sort of seizure.*
> *It turned out afterwards that it was only a*
> *panic attack. I was under a lot of stress at the*
> *time. I was rushed to a hospital, and while I was*
> *waiting for the results of an x-ray, I overheard*
> *the doctor telling someone that I had a pulmo-*
> *nary embolism. I knew enough medical termi-*

nology to know that that meant I was probably about to die. My life didn't flash in front of my face, as you hear so often. I just remember a tremendous feeling of disappointment. There were so many things I wanted to do in my life, and now I wouldn't have the chance. They all involved doing things for others, people I cared about. I wanted them to know how important they were to me. I wanted them to know how much I loved them.

An hour later I was home. Nothing was wrong with me. But the whole experience made a big difference in my life. It's been over twenty years, and I haven't forgotten it. The most important thing to me is to show people I love them, and to try to show it by doing good things for them.

If I had to define my purpose in life in one sentence, I guess that would be it. It must be, because when I thought my life was ending, that was the only thing that was important. I'm glad it happened. When the real thing comes, I think I'll be able to feel that I've done my best.

(Fifty-six-year-old man)

Every story I've heard from people who have thought they were dying is basically the same. They wish they had done more for others, especially those that they love. It must be a basic component of the human spirit. Think about it for yourself. **If you had just one day to live—would you take or would you give?**

What would your life disappointments be if you knew

that there was no more time? What would you most wish you had accomplished? If you had one more chance, to what would you devote your efforts? Make a list. It should give you a good start to begin defining your *purpose*.

Purpose

If you knew that you had just one more day to live:
• What accomplishments in your life would you be proud of?
• What things would you most want to accomplish if you were given one more chance?

Photocopy this chart and keep it in your "Personal Inventory" file.

Accomplishments I'm Proud Of

Goals I Most Want to Accomplish Before I Die

Peace and Contentment—
a "Oneness" with Your Universe

Peace and contentment come from feeling good about yourself, about what you are doing with your life; a feeling of "oneness" with your universe that comes from a sense that you are in the right place at the right time, doing what you were meant to do. Remember that reminiscence about the child in her father's arms? She felt safe and loved and a part of something. That child felt that she was exactly where she was supposed to be.

Many people addicted to alcohol or other drugs have told me how they tried to feed that spiritual hunger for peace and contentment by using chemicals, and how frustrated and confused they felt when the chemicals no longer worked.

I remember sitting on the edge of the bed, time and time again, with my head in my hands, asking, "Why am I like this? I think I'm a good person. I want to do the right thing. I try. Why am I so miserable? There's a big emptiness, a hole in my life. Something's missing."

For a long time, when I felt like that, I'd have a few drinks and then I'd feel OK. I'd feel good about myself, feel like I belonged, like there was hope and that somehow things would turn out all right. Alcohol helped fill that empty hole, but the next time I started drinking, the hole would be bigger and harder to fill. I'd feel even worse when I came out of it. Finally it didn't work at all anymore, and I was left with nothing.

*I think I finally figured it out. There ain't no
such thing as a free lunch, as they say. Alcohol
was giving me the feeling, but I hadn't done
anything to earn it, so the feeling couldn't last
beyond the alcohol. Even worse, my world was
changing while I was medicating my feelings,
so when I would come back to reality, I was
even less prepared to deal with it.*

(Sixty-three-year-old woman)

What we learn from this woman's experience is that her
hunger for feeling at one with the universe was so great that
any way of filling it, even if it was harmful, was better than
living with the emptiness. She had values, she had moral
standards, she wanted to be good, but she couldn't find a
way to meet her own expectations.

It's no accident that the Latin word for alcohol is
spiritus. In most English-speaking countries other than
the United States, "spirits" refers to what Americans call
"liquor" or "hard liquor," drinks that are strong enough to
immediately change the way you feel. When alcohol acts on
the brain, it often brings a relaxed, confident, and peaceful
feeling. Mundane worries suddenly don't seem to be important. It brings peace and contentment—almost the same
feelings that a healthy spirituality brings.

But it's only temporary. It's like a "time-out" from life,
but the world around you changes while you're taking that
time-out. For most people, the occasional use of alcohol is
harmless. Be aware, however, that it won't help you grow,
and if it becomes a substitute for spiritual growth, you
could be headed for disaster.

Look for healthy ways to feel that you're in the right

place, doing the right thing. Think about what you've decided your purposes in life are. Challenge yourself to do at least one thing today, and every day, towards that purpose. It may be a simple act like telling someone that you love them, or phoning a friend who you know is lonely. It may be as personal as a prayer. No day is lost if you have done one thing, no matter how small, that contributes towards your purpose.

Spiritual growth doesn't usually happen in leaps and bounds. It's a slow but steady growth that builds upon small things that you do every day.

The Search for Immortality

It seems that most people yearn for immortality, for some way of living on after earthly existence. It shows itself in many religions as a belief in, or hope for, an afterlife. Other religions or cultures believe in reincarnation or a cycle of life. The veneration of ancestors is a way of having them live on in memory. Works of art, photos, writings, or even carving your initials on a tree—all are ways of leaving behind a sign that you have been here.

Accomplishing something worthwhile in your career can be an important way to leave your mark on the world, a way to live on after you're gone. Be careful to keep balance in your life, though. Excessive devotion to work can also be an addiction—workaholism is the current label. There isn't anything wrong with working hard, doing your best, and trying to accomplish something worthwhile. When I hear people talking about *devotion* to work, however, I get a little bit concerned. Devotion is a word that connotes religious or spiritual dedication.

Maybe it's the difference between striving to do

> *early on I was trying to do the first, to do my best, and I didn't think too much about the competitive aspect. As my career went on, it became more and more important that people considered me the best. More than that, I wanted to think they couldn't get along without me.*
>
> *I remember one morning sitting at my desk at 6:00 A.M. thinking, "Ten years from now, they'll still be saying that I was the best accountant this company ever had." That was going to be one way of being immortal, of living on in people's memories.*
>
> *So I worked and worked, and I got promotions, and people did say I was the best. Looking back, I can say I never got much satisfaction from it, though. I cheated myself because I should have been devoting some of that time to other things. And a year after I retired, it was as if I had never been there.*

(Sixty-six-year-old woman)

There are better ways of feeding your hunger for immortality. The woman who mentored others had it right when she said, "She'll help others, just like my mentor helped me. It will just go on and on and on."

When you help others, whether it be mentoring someone on the job, helping a friend in a time of need, or raising your kids to be responsive to the needs of others, you have started a process that will still be going on long after you're gone.

If you live your life helping only yourself, you might end up like the gentleman in an English churchyard whose

epitaph reads:
> *Here lies a miser who lived for himself*
> *And cared for nothing but gathering pelf*
> *Now where he is or how he fares*
> *Nobody knows, and nobody cares*

Belonging

Your job may have provided various ways to satisfy the need to belong, to be part of something worthwhile. If you fill that need in other ways through church, family, or by working with groups or organizations, your new freedom in retirement can be a blessing. If work was your main source of belonging, though, you're likely to feel isolated.

> *I wasn't all that dedicated to my job, although people thought I was because I was always there. I came early and left late. I didn't take vacation days until my boss insisted on it. I neither liked nor disliked my job, but when I was there at least I felt like I was somebody. I didn't realize it, but it had become my only connection to the world, so when I had to face retirement it was really scary.*

(Sixty-three-year-old man)

This need to belong, if it's without a spiritual component, can sometimes lead to frantic socialization. You may find yourself constantly engaging in activities that have no meaning, purpose, or value for you, just because they provide an opportunity for you to be with other people.

> *I was out somewhere just about every night. I had to have people around me in order to feel like I was part of the world. It didn't work, though. That phrase "feeling lonely in a crowded*

room" sure applied to me.

(Sixty-two-year-old man)

If you're trying to get a sense of belonging from your job, or from frantic socializing, you'd better look for other ways to fill that need in the years to come. If you've got family ties, try to find ways to strengthen them. If you belong to a church, start participating in activities that work towards the kind of purpose you believe in. Seek out volunteer opportunities that will put you in touch with others who are working towards the same purposes. If you don't belong to a church, try to find one that meets your needs. Shop around.

Try to learn more about other people, other religions, and other cultures. It's difficult to understand your place in the scheme of things if you know nothing about the rest of the universe. Making a real connection with others, understanding them, and working with them towards a common goal are the best ways to satisfy that need to belong.

Wonder and Worship

Perhaps the culmination of all these spiritual hungers we've discussed is a need to believe in something greater than yourself. This hunger embraces the need to have a purpose, a power, or a plan that transcends individual human life. For most people who are reading this book, that need is filled by a belief in God, gods, or a spirit world. I wouldn't be so presumptuous as to try to tell you what you should believe in. I was taught the Ten Commandments of the Judeo-Christian tradition, and to be so arrogant as to believe I could define God for someone else would be an affront to the first commandment. I do believe, though, that you will be more fulfilled if you can open your mind to the glory and beauty of the world we live in. Many faiths believe that standing in awe of creation is the greatest form of worship. Go into the world of nature and let yourself be overwhelmed by the beauty of creation. Read the great works of literature and marvel at the beauty and strength of the human spirit. Listen to Beethoven's *The Glory of God in Nature.* Read a book on astronomy, or better yet, look at the skies through a telescope and appreciate the incomprehensible vastness of the universe. It will help you understand what a tiny part of creation you are. At the same time, you will appreciate your significance in being part of such a vast and wonderful creation.

Spiritual Needs

• Think about your spiritual needs—like belonging, sense of purpose, being needed, immortality, etc.

• Examine how you fill those needs now, in ways that may be healthy or unhealthy.

Photocopy this chart and keep it in your "Personal Inventory" file.

Spiritual Needs	Healthy Ways	Unhealthy Ways

5

Being Somebody

Understanding Your Identity

I ran into Bob at a concert. I hadn't seen him since he had retired from a large corporation six months earlier. He had a highly successful career and was known and respected not only in his own community, but nationally and internationally as well. "Bob," I said, "I'm teaching a preretirement seminar next week for your old company, and I need a good opener. How about putting into one sentence the most significant effect that retirement has had for you?" Bob answered without hesitation. "In twenty-four hours," he said, "I went from 'Who's Who' to 'Who's He?'"

I know Bob fairly well, and I think he's got his life in balance. *He* knows who he is, and to him, that's what's important. But if he had been someone who based all of his self-identity on the extent to which the rest of the world admired his accomplishments, going from "Who's Who" to "Who's He?" could have been devastating.

Who are you? If someone wanted to really understand and appreciate what a unique human being you are, what should they know about you? They'd need to know what your values are, what you believe in, what you think your purpose in living is, what you think you need to do with your life in order to fulfill that purpose, and what you're doing about it.

They'd also want to know about your relationships with others, and why they are important to you. What have you done in your life that you feel was really worthwhile, and why do you think so? What do you do with your time now? What are your aspirations for the future? If you could choose to do whatever you wanted, what would it be? When you are gone, what would you most like to be remembered for? These are fundamental questions that will help you define your unique identity. That's going to be essential as you prepare to make your life more satisfying—now and during retirement.

In our society, we frequently define ourselves and others by a job, profession, or role, and the titles and activities that go along with it. Watch what happens at the next social gathering you attend. When people who haven't met before are trying to become acquainted, the conversation seldom goes on for more than a few minutes before one or the other asks the question, "What do you do?" If you give a job title, the other person is able to classify you, to put you into a neat little box that will largely govern how the conversation goes from that point on. In turn, that makes you comfortable, because those are the terms you've grown accustomed to using to describe yourself.

But let's admit it—this is terribly limiting! If you need a job title to define who you are, you must not be much. And if your job activities are the primary source of your identity now, who are you going to be when the job is no longer a part of your life?

Is what you do to earn a living what you are? Of course not, but if you want to run a little test just to see how far we've fallen into this trap, try saying, "I'm retired." The next question will most likely be, "What did you used to do?", as if life after the job is non-existent.

To better understand your spiritual identity you examined such issues as what you believe your purpose in life is, your moral values, and what you feel you need to do to meet that purpose and those values. You also need to know your personal identity. Mencius said, "He who knows his essential nature, knows heaven."

Personal and spiritual identity are intertwined, of course, but your personal identity has more to do with how you see your role in the world, how you interact with others, and how they see you. It's based on the activities you pursue to try to satisfy those spiritual values you've identified. It's about how you set goals and what kind of rewards you get from meeting them. It's how you feel about yourself, and why you feel that way.

Being Somebody

When you're in basic training in the army, you don't have much in the way of status or identity. I had a friend from Oklahoma who'd come up to me on Saturday night and say, "Let's go get drunk and *be* somebody!" Well, getting drunk wasn't a very effective, healthy, or lasting way to feel self-worth, but the story illustrates that everyone has a need to feel that they are somebody, and that they have a place in this world, a reason for being, and an identity.

There are different ways to define your identity, and some of them come from your job. It's important to understand where your feelings of identity come from now, so that as some of those sources disappear, you'll know what you have to do to maintain feelings of self-worth.

Sources of Identity

Some cultures establish your identity for you. It doesn't make much difference what you do, how you think, or what you accomplish. Identity is based on rank or lineage. If your parents are of the nobility, then you are, too. Lineage might even be reflected in your name, like Pederson or Pedersdottir. Everyone knows you're a descendant of Peder, and that's all they need to know to figure out who and what you are.

Even in a supposedly classless society like ours, this kind of identification exists more than we would like to admit. Here it's based on wealth rather than lineage, although in some families who have been wealthy for generations, their name alone forms a large part of their identity. Think of what your immediate impression would be if you met someone named Rockefeller. You would likely make several assumptions even though you knew little about them. This *aristocratic* approach to identity causes some problems, especially for the people who bear the name of wealthy or famous families.

> *I once sat in the office of a good friend, whose name was well-known and associated with wealth. He was on the receiving end of a flattering phone call. When he hung up he turned to me and said, "Sometimes I wish I wasn't rich. You never know whether people are being nice to you because you deserve it, or because they want something from you."*

I've had the opportunity to know both the very rich and the very poor. It's hard sometimes for the rich to feel a sense of personal accomplishment. They may be doing some real good, but they don't know if they're being asked to help because people want their personal involvement, or whether people are just interested in using their name or their money. For the most part, the poor have a much clearer idea of who they really are. They get more honest feedback from the rest of the world.

(Fifty-five-year-old man)

Is name, wealth, or social status one of your sources of identity? There's nothing wrong with that, but you may feel that by itself it's not fulfilling enough. If you have inherited wealth or a famous name, or are the beneficiary of profits you gain from ownership in an enterprise, it can be difficult to have a feeling of purpose in life unless you truly understand how your role fits in with the lives of those people who created, or are creating that wealth. Those are the people who are out there every day, doing the work that contributes to the success and profitability of the enterprise. If you get involved with them, you'll not only feel better about yourself, you'll understand your role in the world better.

If you're one of those who feel like you've been credited for your name or your money, try to look for ways to get involved in worthwhile projects that use your skills instead. Get down in the trenches and work with the people who are really involved with implementing a project. Give yourself, not just your assets, to something you believe in.

I'd been giving $10,000 a year to a shelter for the homeless. I was sure it was worthwhile, and

I got some satisfaction from it. I even helped raise more funds in the community, but I found myself feeling a little resentful each year when they'd come back asking for more.

Then the director managed to get me to spend a couple of hours down there one day, mainly to convince me the money was being well-spent. It was a different world, one I'd never really seen. She convinced me that I ought to volunteer to work in the food line once in a while. It took some urging, but I finally tried it. It's been the greatest learning experience of my life. I've really gotten to know some of those people. I was uncomfortable at first, but they weren't.

Now I realize that those folks who are coming through the food line are every bit as good as me or you; they're just having a tougher time of it. I don't know if I could do as well under the circumstances. I've made some good friends, and they're just as important to me as my friends at the country club. It's given me a whole new outlook on people, and I like myself better as a result.

I really look forward to my Wednesday nights down at the shelter. OK, I'll admit I sometimes sneak down on the weekends too, just to see how things are going. And I still give the money. In fact, I've increased the amount because I know what it's doing, but now I do it anony-mously. It's a lot more fun that way. Besides, I'm more proud of the work I do there than I am of the money I give. I feel like this is something that I was meant to do. When I'm gone, I'd rather be remembered as someone who was a friend, rather than for the donations.

(Forty-nine-year-old man)

Recognition

Another way we identify ourselves is by the recognition we get from others. Most social scientists refer to American society as a *meritocracy*. This means that you're judged, classified, or identified as a worthwhile human being depending on what you have accomplished, and how others view your accomplishments. Recognition also helps fill the wish for immortality. We hope that our deeds might somehow live on in someone's memory. It leaves a mark that we have been here.

Basing identity on recognition has some drawbacks, however. When you act to impress others, you're making a statement that you think your own judgment isn't worth much, that you have to rely on the judgment of others to determine if you're worthwhile. Also, the kind of accomplishments that you're recognized for are often materialistic in nature and usually related to work, rather than other parts of your life.

This doesn't mean that work that achieves some materialistic standard is inherently bad. You may be working to achieve goals that are important to your own values, and that work may result in profit or other success. What's more important to your identity, though, is *why* you're doing that work. If it results in material gain, so much the better for you, and perhaps others. Success aside, you'll feel content only if what you're doing meets your own standards. If you judge yourself against standards set by society, you might gain the world's acclaim and wonder why you don't like yourself very much.

It's so much more personally rewarding to be giving something of yourself because of what you believe in, rather than what the rest of the world might think. It's said that a wealthy American tourist, being taken on a tour of Calcutta to observe the poor living conditions, stopped to watch Mother Teresa as she was cleaning the sores of a leper. "I couldn't do that for a million dollars," he said. Mother Teresa kept right on working. Without looking up, she said, "Neither could I."

You'll feel the greatest satisfaction when you do something because it's worth doing, not because there might be a payoff or recognition.

If you've been getting your identity from the recognition of your job accomplishments, you'll probably lose that source when you retire. You're either going to have to rest on your laurels or find other ways to gain recognition. If you're going to rest on your laurels and try to survive on the recognition of past accomplishments, you'd do well to take a look at what you're being recognized for.

> *I've been giving a lot of thought as to how I'd like to be remembered in this company after I'm gone, and I've thought about how we talk about people who left years ago. Remember Carol? You never hear anyone mention that she was our leading salesperson seven years in a row. No, they talk about how great she was at developing her subordinates, and how many people got their start because of her.*
>
> *And Charlie? People don't remember what a*

great engineer he was, just that he was the
meanest son of a bitch they ever worked for.

(Forty-seven-year-old woman)

Chances are, you'll be remembered for character, principle, and how you treated others, not for the profit or loss you made. That's not to diminish the importance of the material things you've accomplished—they might have been significant and had worth of their own. Just don't expect to be remembered for them.

Comparison

A third way we form our identity is by comparing ourselves with others. This usually becomes a competitive formula.

I'd like to judge myself by my own standards.
That's how I believe it should be done. It's what
I tell other people to do. Emotionally, though,
I know I just don't do it. If something tells me
that someone else is being judged as better
than me in any way, I feel inferior. I remember
early in my career, I had quite a reputation in
the industry. I would get good job offers from
other companies. I liked where I was, but I
would apply for those other jobs just to see
what kind of response I would get. I had no
intention of accepting, but if I wasn't offered
the job, I'd be highly offended. It's ridiculous, I
know, but it hurt me to think that they had
found someone they thought was better
than me.

We're told that doing your best is what's impor-
tant, but we're showed that comparison with

> *others is how it's going to be measured. I was a*
> *pretty good student. In grade school I'd bring*
> *home a report card that was mostly A's. I'd*
> *show it to Dad, and instead of praising the A's,*
> *he'd ask, "Were you first in the class?"*

(Forty-six-year-old man)

If you use this competitive model to value yourself, you can't possibly win. There will always be someone who appears to be not doing as well, so you can look down on them with false superiority. That's unkind, and it's usually inaccurate. The other side of the coin is that there will always be someone who seems to be doing better than you, so you'll always feel inferior. You might also rob yourself of the enjoyment that comes from doing something just because you enjoy it, even though you might not be the best at it. Here's a good example:

> *When I was a kid, I was a very good musician.*
> *I was the best pianist in my school, and for my*
> *age, the best in town. I got a lot of enjoyment*
> *from playing. Even though I didn't think of it in*
> *competitive terms, I'm sure I enjoyed knowing*
> *that I was the best in my little world. That*
> *continued through high school. I couldn't go to*
> *college at first for financial reasons but at age*
> *twenty-one I finally did, and I decided to major*
> *in music.*
>
> *The very first week of school I discovered that*
> *of the twenty people in my class, all were at*
> *least as talented as me, and most had better*
> *training. For the first time in my life I wasn't*
> *the best musician. In fact, I was in the lowest*
> *third of the group. It was devastating, and I*

didn't know how to handle it. I dropped out of school, and I didn't touch the piano for three years. Of course, I grew up and realized that you don't have to be a star to enjoy music, and now I play a lot for my own enjoyment. Still, I could have robbed myself of that pleasure if I had given up just because I wasn't the greatest.

(Fifty-five-year-old man)

If you've judged yourself by measuring your accomplishments against others, you'll have a dilemma when you enter a stage in life where there isn't any way to keep score. You've probably heard people say that some of the most unhappy people are former sports heroes who didn't develop other facets of themselves. They got all of their self-worth from the adulation they received in their sports role, and then felt like they were nobody when they had to move into the "real world."

If you're committed to what you believe is your purpose in life, and feel that you are clear on what your values are, you're in a good position to start judging your accomplishments against your own standards, instead of competing. You'll only have to keep score against yourself.

It's difficult to get away from thinking in competitive terms because it's probably been a major part of your life, but it can be done. During retirement, you'll have more control over your life than you did throughout your employment years. You won't have to do things to please or impress others. It will be easier to have the courage to be yourself, rather than being what you need to be to impress others. You can start giving yourself credit for improvement and for progress, rather than for being the best.

What you want to be, what you believe in, and how you

are striving to achieve your purpose in life, is what you are. This is your character. What others think of you is your reputation. Ask yourself which is more important to you at this time of life—your character or your reputation. If it's character, start judging yourself by measuring whether you're making progress according to your own values, and stop worrying about what others think.

>*It wasn't until late in life that I finally figured out that it didn't make much sense to be worried about what others thought about my success. I really didn't have much control over that. Sure, you try to do your best, but there's still a huge element of luck, either good or bad, that determines whether you're successful or not in your career. What I do have control over is my character, my standards, and those are the things that make me what I am.*

>*I think I always had pretty good standards for myself, even though I couldn't always articulate them very well. But through most of my life, as I look back now, I was judging myself, at least a lot of the time, by the feedback I was getting from others. I think most people do that. It's like you're an actor, and you don't know whether you're good unless you're getting applause. So you keep modifying the act until the audience applauds, whether the audience is friends, family, or co-workers. That's probably okay some of the time—I know I need feedback—but I ended up believing that I was the role that I was playing. I wasn't being me.*

Now, I think I know who I am, and it's not all that different from the role I played. Now the applause that counts is that which I give myself when I can honestly believe I'm living up to my values. And by golly, I don't mind saying that I do it a good share of the time!

I went through life always kind of sad and disappointed that I didn't achieve my childhood dreams. Lately I've figured out that my childhood dreams were all based on fame and fortune, all that competitive stuff again. If I look one step beyond that, though, the childhood dreams were also based on what I wanted to do: to achieve something worthwhile, and to do some good. Now that I judge myself against my own values, I know I did some things that were worthwhile. The child I used to be thought that should result in fame and fortune. The adult I am now tells me that what matters is whether I did some good. I find that I did achieve a lot of those dreams, even though I didn't get the acclaim. Now, it doesn't matter, because I'm pretty content with myself.

(Sixty-seven-year-old woman)

Moral Identity

An important part of self-worth is your perception of yourself as a good person, someone who is doing what is right or moral. Part of that feeling comes from feedback you get on the job—performance reviews, conforming to work standards, and acceptance from friends and co-workers. Feedback acts as a mirror in which you can see yourself as others see you. Without that mirror, you might find it more difficult to feel confidence in your actions, even though what you're doing may be right.

> *Years ago I was the target of a false accusation at work. My friends and co-workers, who knew I was incapable of such behavior, immediately rallied around me in support and even outrage. That gave me the strength and confidence to face the accusation until it was proved false. Last year I had a misunderstanding with an old friend, something not very serious, actually. It was a private matter and one that I really didn't want to discuss with anyone. I found myself waking up in the middle of the night, feeling guilty about something I hadn't even done. I didn't have any way of checking out my own feelings as to whether I was right or wrong. My friend and I straightened out the problem. Neither of us was wrong, but it was awfully confusing there for a while.*

(Sixty-four-year-old man)

It's going to be important to maintain some of the external reference points that your job provided. Find someone that you trust with whom you can talk openly when you're feeling unsure of your judgment. Church membership or association with others who share your moral values are other ways of holding up that mirror to see yourself as others see you.

Being Needed

Another source of identity is a feeling of being needed by others. It's great to feel that a person, group, or enterprise can't get along without you. That makes you feel important. It also fills another basic need, to feel that you're part of something larger than yourself.

Before the advent of anti-depressant medication in the late 1950s, mental hospitals admitted a large number of patients under a diagnosis you don't hear much about anymore. It was called *involutional melancholia,* a form of depression. Patients with this diagnosis were usually in their forties or fifties. For women, under the stereotypes of the time, it was often called the *empty nest syndrome.* That term was meant to describe the feeling of uselessness or meaninglessness that came after the patient had completed her "main role in life," in this case raising the kids. Now she felt that she had no further usefulness in the world. She wasn't needed anymore.

Your job provided a feeling of belonging and being needed. You were part of something, a company, and worked together with others towards a common goal. You needed each other. If that's been a significant source of your self-worth, not being needed on the job can be pretty traumatic. Whether you were the president of the company or an assembly line worker, there was always a feeling of being needed by others. Your co-workers depended on you to be there, if nothing else. There were parts of the job you knew better than anyone else. You probably believed that certain tasks just couldn't be done quite as well without you.

> *I didn't think they could run the place without me. Oh, intellectually, I'd tell myself that of course they could. Others had left and the company somehow managed to go on, but emotionally, I didn't think things could possi-*

bly be the same if I wasn't there. And rationally, I knew so much about my part of the business that I was sure they'd still want my input on things after I left. It would be a waste of resources if they didn't continue to use what I knew.

Managers at the company seemed to agree. In discussions about my impending retirement they'd talk about how they'd need my input. They asked if it was OK if they called me for help. We even discussed some formal consulting arrangements.

That made my leaving easier. I would still be a part of the company, just playing a different role. But they never called. Oh, I got some friendly calls, especially at first. I'd keep waiting for them to ask for help, and all they'd ask about was how I was doing. I'd ask about how some projects were going, hoping they'd ask for advice. They'd just give me a brief report on how well it was going.

I'd come home a couple times a day and check my answering machine, expecting a call for help. It never came. I'd drop in at the office, ostensibly just to say hello. I figured if they saw me, they'd remember all the things I did and ask my opinion. Instead, they'd exchange pleasantries and imply that they were envious of my life of leisure.

I'd wake up in the middle of the night feeling depressed, angry, and resentful. It took me a while to identify just where those feelings were coming from. Nobody needed me! Or, worse yet, they did need me but they were rejecting me! They just didn't want me around anymore!

(Sixty-six-year-old man)

It's ironic that they probably do need you, or at least could profit from continuing to call on your experience and expertise. But the fact is, it isn't done that way, at least in most western businesses. Sometimes this is a vestige of the attitude of thirty years ago that younger is better. More often, it's a symptom of a cultural issue that has long been a problem for western management—an inability to deal with ambiguity. Things have to be either black or white, with no gray allowed. You're either an employee or you're retired, you can't be both. It might not be fair, and it isn't smart business, but it's the way it is.

It wasn't until I really accepted the fact that I was no longer part of the business, that they were going to get along without me for better or worse, that I was able to get on with my life and put myself into other things wholeheartedly. Maybe it would have helped if there had been a more formal end to things at work. I declined a retirement party because I didn't like being the center of attention. Besides, I was afraid I would choke up. In retrospect, it might have helped the transition. It would have been a way for me and the company to say good-bye to each other. Someone once told me that life was a process of closing old doors and opening new ones. I tried to open a new door without closing the old one. It didn't work.

You need to decide when it's time to put an end to one stage of your life. Usually, when you leave a particular job, that's the end of that episode. You don't want to accept it, and the people you are leaving want to make you feel good, so they also look for ways to avoid it. But in most cases, that's the way it is. Close the door and get on with something else. To do otherwise will just prolong the agony. Don't tell yourself that in your case, it's going to be different. Chances are, it won't be.

You'll need to find some other ways to feel needed. There are plenty of them out there, and some real rewards await you if you seek them out. Don't expect to feel needed unless you have something to offer that will fulfill an existing need. It's not going to just come to you, you have to be willing to seek out opportunities to give of yourself.

Being needed, feeling that you can somehow contribute to the welfare of others, is part of being loved. It's a basic human instinct. Just because no one is telling you that they need you, doesn't mean no one needs you. As long as you have anything to offer, someone out there appreciates you. Much of what you identify as need before you retire, might just be dependency. How much more rewarding it will be for you if you can identify some real needs in the world, and answer them. Believe me, the needs are out there.

If you're planning a second career, look for jobs that will give you the chance to be of service to others. Social service agencies, schools, and nursing homes are often looking for both full-time and part-time employees. Check out the volunteer needs in your community. I mean now, not after you've retired. It's not just an opportunity to be needed or to contribute, it's a chance to do new things and discover new talents and interests. I've found that the people who feel most rewarded by volunteerism are those who are doing things they never thought they could do, and helping others in the process. Open a new door, and let someone in that needs you.

> *I started doing some volunteer work, tutoring kids in an inner city school. Reading—imagine that! I think those kids actually look forward to the morning they spend with me. In a small way, I'm part of their life. Even if they didn't appreciate it, if I thought that I helped them in any way, I'd feel like I contributed to the world. In fact, I feel that way now. I'm part of that school, part of the community, and part of an effort to help the disadvantaged. I feel prouder of that than I ever did about being part of the company.*

> (Sixty-two-year-old woman)

Belonging

> *If someone had told me ten years ago that I had a messed up sense of identity, I would have either laughed or gotten angry. Either way, I would have thought that they were the one that was messed up, not me. But now I know that I was wrong. My job had become my family, my church. My goals were job goals, my standards were work standards. Oh, not entirely, of course, but my job was really a larger part of my whole being than anything else. Association with others at work was my community.*
> *Then suddenly, and I mean suddenly, even*

though I had quite a bit of time to prepare for it, I wasn't part of that community any more. Somehow, I never figured on that. I don't know what I expected, but I know that as it began to sink in that I was out of there, it really hurt. It was like being thrown out of your family. As far as the company went, it was as though I had never been.

If only I had gotten some balance in my life and my priorities years ago. I thought I had it, though. I think it's something wrong with our society, that it would seem natural to get so much of your feeling of identity from your job. If I had had better balance back then, I would have gotten more out of life, and retirement would have been a joy instead of a kick in the butt. And you know what? I would have been a better employee, too. I finally figured it out, though, and I'm lucky. I didn't alienate my family or anything like that. I just feel bad that I didn't do more when I could have, and I'm trying to make up for it now.

(Fifty-eight-year-old man)

Everyone needs a feeling of belonging. That's why it can be so devastating if you feel like you've been "thrown out" of the group, as can happen if you've been laid off, forced out of work by cutbacks, or pushed into early retirement.

You need to search for activities and associations to satisfy the need to feel like you have a certain place in the world that only you can fill. In order to do that, you should have a clear understanding of how you are filling that need now. If most of your sense of belonging comes from your job, it's time to start finding outside activities.

If you want to regain or strengthen that feeling of belonging, of being part of something meaningful, then you're going to have to reach out. It's not likely that opportunities will come to you, or just happen. The way to reach out is not to ask to be taken in, but to give something of yourself that is needed. Find ways to be of value to others. There are many needs out there, and you have something to offer. Your task is to find the place where you can make the best contribution.

Many people have found that chance through volunteerism, others through their church, community groups, or charities. It may be as simple as calling someone that you know is lonely or neglected, visiting a nursing home, or soliciting funds for your church, but it must be done in the spirit of trying to help others, not looking for acceptance or reward.

Sources of Identity

- What are your sources of identity now?
- Where do they come from?
- How are they likely to change in the next few years?
- How will you replace them?

Photocopy this chart and keep it in your "Personal Inventory" file.

Source of Identity

continued on next page

Sources of Identity...

Source of Identity *(continued)*

_____

Where I Find My Identity Now

_____

Where I'll Find My Identity in the Future

_____

6

You Can Be What You Always Wanted To Be

An Opportunity for Personal Growth

After examining your sources of spiritual and personal identity, you should have a basic understanding of where your feelings of self-worth come from. You may have decided that you've been short-changing yourself and that you'd like to do some other things with your life. Or, you may be satisfied with your identity as it is, but have some concerns about how your needs are going to be met in the future.

Maybe you'd like to expand your horizons, getting involved in new activities without giving up your old ones. Maybe you'd just like to improve yourself. All of those objectives are worthwhile, but it's up to you to decide which ones you want to pursue. This chapter will provide some guidelines to help you decide where you want to go, and how to get there.

Please be patient
God's not finished with me yet.

You've probably heard someone make that statement, implying that they're hoping to become a better person than they are now. Putting all the responsibility on God, though, doesn't seem fair. Miracles are more likely to happen if you're putting some effort into the project yourself. Sam's story is a good example:

When Sam bought the old farm, it was in total disrepair. The yard was overgrown with weeds, and the buildings were falling apart. Sam worked diligently, repairing and painting the buildings, cleaning up the yard, mending the fence, planting shrubs and flowers. From time to time the local parson would stop by, admire Sam's work for awhile, then say, "Sam, it's just amazing what you and the Lord are doing with this place." Finally, Sam couldn't take it any more. This time he replied, "Parson, you should have seen this place when the Lord had it all to himself."

Sam realized that if he was going to improve his situation in life, he was going to have to assume responsibility and take some action.

For much of your life, you may have been too weighed down with responsibility, the need to earn a paycheck and put bread on the table, to devote much time to improving yourself. You also might have had some misconceptions about what was possible. We all want to improve. If that's your goal, then anything's possible. You might not master a new field, but if, through your efforts, you know more about it than you did before, then you've improved, and you've met your goal. But if you want to change, expand your horizons and improve yourself, you're going to have to take responsibility and get on with the project. Taking action now can be fun, exciting, and rewarding.

Many people have told me that they've gone through life always wondering if they were doing what they were meant to do, what they had been put on earth to accomplish. Others say that they're afraid to strive for what they really want to be, because they think pursuing a personal mission sounds too grandiose. Others fear that they might try for it and fail. If you try to reach some goal and don't get there, is that failure? It's not, if you've learned something in the process.

> *This counselor kept trying to convince me to go to college and get my degree, now that the kids were in school and I had some time. All I could think of was that I'd put in all that time, maybe go to college for two or three years, and either not be able to finish, or flunk out. It would make me look foolish. "Kate," I'd say, "I'm thirty-four years old. I'll be thirty-eight when I graduate!" I kept looking at college as a four year chunk of time that would be wasted if I didn't earn a degree. Two years later I was saying, "Kate, I'm thirty-six years old. I'll be forty years old when I graduate!"*

> *Then one day Kate stopped me. "Mary," she said, "how old will you be four years from now if you* don't *go to college? That one got me, I admit. The point, obviously, was that time was going to continue on whether I was doing anything for myself or not.*

> *Well, I quit thinking about college as a four year chunk of time with a degree at the end, and started thinking about it as a challenge to do something that I wanted to do. I enrolled with the attitude that I'd try it for a semester*

and just find out what it was like. It turned out that I loved it and for the next three years I went because I was enjoying the experience, the learning, and the self-confidence that went with it. The degree was no longer important; it wasn't the objective any more—self-improvement was. I did get my college degree, and I'm proud of that. But I'm even more proud of what I've done for myself. Now, twenty years later, I still take a course about once a year, just because learning something new makes me feel good about myself.

(Sixty-one-year-old woman)

You may have grown up with the wrong perspective on what's possible in the way of self-improvement. Our culture is responsible for some of that. Do you remember the fairy tales you heard as a child? Usually the hero or heroine struggled through hardships until the climax of the story and then... "they lived happily ever after." The message was that life was an uphill struggle to a certain point. Then after that, everything was great. You had to improve yourself to a certain level, and then you could coast the rest of your life.

Our social system encourages this kind of thinking, too. You work through a certain level of education, then you get a job. You advance to a certain level in your career, then you stay there the rest of your life. Or worse, you get to a certain level and think, "Well, I've gone as far as I'm going; it's probably all downhill from here." You tend to think that early in life all your options are open, and late in life they're all closing.

Neither of these views is correct, of course. Even early in life some options were never open to you, limited by your inherent abilities. If you're five feet tall, you probably never really had the option of being an all-star center on a professional basketball team. Conversely, in later life, some options do close down. If you're sixty-five and your golf score is 132, it's not likely that you're ever going to win the U.S. Open golf championship. But if you're working on the process of personal growth, and if you're continuing to make better use of the abilities you do have, you're constantly opening up new options for yourself, more than are closing down.

Personal Restructuring

A business restructures so it can be competitive and profitable in a changing marketplace. A company decides where it wants to be in the market, and analyzes its resources. Then it decides how to apply those resources in the most effective way to achieve its new goals. You should use the same process as you approach retirement.

Decide In Which Direction You Want to Grow

If you want to make the best use of your future personal growth, you first need to decide in which direction you want to grow. What are your goals? What do you want to do with the rest of your life? What kind of rewards will you need in order to feel that you're getting the most out of life? What kind of activities bring you personal satisfaction now? Do they produce the kind of rewards that you say you want?

Analyze Your Resources

Start your personal restructuring process by taking an inventory. The purpose of this inventory is to clearly define for yourself just what it is you like doing, what you're good at, and what kind of rewards you want from life. It should help you understand yourself better, and give you some guidance as to how you will need to proceed.

As you put together this inventory (see chart on opposite page), it's important that you be brutally honest with yourself. The purpose is to paint a picture of the real you, not what you'd like others to think you are. Some people are reluctant to put down things like money, power, or control as desired rewards, because they think it doesn't sound good. If those are really your goals, though, you're probably not going to be too happy if you don't achieve them.

This exercise is to try to help you decide what you like to do, what you're good at, and what you want for a reward. Put down everything that comes to mind. You can narrow it down later. There are no right or wrong answers. You're simply defining yourself.

First, take a look at the "Personal Inventory" chart. Photocopy it and keep coming back and making additions to it. As you go through this process, you'll find your horizons expanding.

Start by entering in the "Activity" column things that you do now—both on the job and in your leisure time.

In describing what you do, don't use job-related terms. For example, if you're a front line supervisor, don't say, "I supervise workers on an assembly line." Instead, say, "I motivate people to work together," or, "I help people get along with one another, and to improve themselves. I do this and this to help them accomplish their goals and make their work more enjoyable."

If you're one of the people working on the assembly line, instead of "I put together widgets," you can say, "I work

Personal Inventory

Activity	Enjoyment Rating (1–5)	Skill Level (G, N, P)	Reward

with others to accomplish a common goal." If you're a manager, you might be able to say, "I coordinate the efforts of many people to reach a common goal."

Try to spell out the activities as they relate to dealing with others, or accomplishing a purpose. Stay away from job-related terms, financial objectives, or end products. You're trying to describe what you're doing at some given point in time, not what you're trying to accomplish. Practice this for awhile, and you'll find it becomes easier. You'll probably end up with some general observations like this:

> *I socialize with others.*
>
> *I follow a routine. I arrive for my work or for other appointments on time.*
>
> *I work with details and keep things orderly.*
>
> *I persuade people to try new things.*
>
> *I try to make others comfortable.*
>
> *I try to help people improve themselves.*
>
> *I use unplanned leisure time to simply relax.*
>
> *I read.*
>
> *I learn new things and new skills.*
>
> *I try to increase my understanding of myself and others.*
>
> *I spend time doing things with members of my family.*
>
> *I use my skills to teach others.*
>
> *I solve problems.*
>
> *I play golf. I go to concerts. I watch TV. I visit with neighbors.*

Make an exhaustive list in the "Activities" column of your "Personal Inventory." Keep coming back and adding to it for a few weeks. If you're having trouble developing the list, carry a small notebook and from time to time during the day, jot down what you're doing at a given moment. Keep in mind that you must describe what activity is taking place. Don't describe it as a job function or as what you're trying to accomplish.

After you've developed a thorough list of activities, the next task is to identify those things you most enjoy doing. You need to focus on individual activities, not projects or jobs. That's why you're doing this exercise, to help you clearly identify for yourself the activities that bring the most joy to your life.

Go through your list and give each activity a score in the "Enjoyment Rating" column.

"I really enjoy this activity, life would be pretty dull without it." Score 1.

"I enjoy this activity, I'd like to continue doing something like it." Score 2.

"This is a pleasant activity, but I could do without it if I had enough of the first two." Score 3.

"This activity is not something I enjoy. I'd rather not do it if I didn't have to." Score 4.

"It would be great if I never had to do this again in my life." Score 5.

Columns 1 and 2 define your *interest pattern*. Obviously, life would be more fun if you could spend all your time doing those things you enjoy the most, the 1s and 2s, and eliminate those activities you don't like. That's not possible all the time, but you should have more opportunity to choose in the future, especially after retirement. If you've really defined your interests, with a little planning and creativity you should be able to find some immediate ways to incorporate more of those 1s and 2s into your daily activities.

Now, do a performance review on yourself. For each activity, give yourself a grade in the "Skill Level" column.

Give yourself a G if you're good at it.

Give yourself an N if you need to improve your skills to do it really well.

Give yourself a P if you're poor at this.

You've just defined your *skills*. You'll get more satisfaction and an increased feeling of self-worth from doing those things that you enjoy, if you are able to do them well. If you've got some activities on your list that earned an enjoyment rating of 1, but your skill level for that activity is an N or P, you can find enjoyment through education, training, experience, or other ways, to improve your skills.

In the "Reward" column, try to define why you enjoy that particular activity and why it's important to you.

It may be as simple as sheer exuberance in the exercise you get from playing golf, or something as profound as feeling that teaching others improves the condition of the world, thus fulfilling some of your spiritual goals. Any response is OK, but it might take some thought on your part to clearly define for yourself just why your favorite activities are meaningful and important to you. You may end up with something like this:

> *I learn from this, and I feel like I'm improving myself.*
> *It gives me a chance to be with other people.*
> *It's exciting.*
> *I can be creative.*
> *It makes me feel important.*
> *I have a chance to help others.*
> *It's a way of showing my love for my family.*
> *I like to make decisions.*

It's a way of having power.
I make money doing it.
I like to be the one in charge.
It's a way of being part of something without having to take responsibility.
I like to be the center of attention.
It makes me feel like I'm doing what I was put on earth to do.
It fills some of my spiritual goals.
I think it makes the world a better place for everyone.

What you're doing is defining the *rewards* you need in order to feel like you're getting the most out of your life. This column will probably be the most difficult, but it is also the most important to your future happiness.

Now take a look at all the activities to which you gave a 1 or 2 "Enjoyment Rating." Where do you find the opportunity to do these things now? And where will you do them in the future? Some of your responses might include: on my job, from my hobbies, work with my church or community group, with family or friends, alone, from recreational activities, etc.

Photocopy and complete the "Blueprint for Your Future" chart on page 125 and include it with your "Personal Inventory" file.

If most of the activities that earned an enjoyment rating of 1 or 2 are now fulfilled on your job, you're lucky—for now. But what are you going to do if your job changes, or you retire? You need to start looking for ways to incorporate these enjoyable activities into other areas of your life.

On the other hand, if you now find your most enjoyable activities are away from the job, you probably will have an easier time adjusting to retirement. You might be short-changing yourself right now, though, because there may be ways to incorporate more of these enjoyable activities into your current work. It might even help you perform better on the job. You're usually more effective and better motivated when you're doing things you enjoy.

Once you've pinpointed where most of your enjoyable activities come from now, you need to start planning how you'll replace those interests and rewards as the pattern of your life changes. You may have to look for new opportunities to use the skills and interests you intend to develop in the future. Most likely, opportunities exist to provide these activities, but you need to find out about them.

If you want to be in the job market, there's a wonderful publication put out by the United States government called the *Occupational Outlook Handbook*. It describes a wide range of occupations, tells you what kind of skills, training, or experience they call for and whether there is a demand for these skills. It gives you an idea of where to look for opportunities and where to get more information. It even gives you an idea of what kind of salary to expect. It's updated yearly and can be found in the reference section of most public libraries.

If you think your interests fit a particular kind of job, you might ask someone in that occupation if they'd be willing to talk with you about what they do. These are often called "informational interviews." Most people are willing or even flattered if you ask them to spend thirty minutes telling you about what they do, especially if they understand you're not looking for an employment interview.

Contact your local charitable organizations or churches to find out what they need in the way of volunteer or paid

Blueprint for Your Future

Enjoyable Activity *	Where I Find It Now	Where I'll Find It in the Future

* Activities you gave an "Enjoyment Rating" of 1 or 2

part-time work that might fit your skills and interests. You'll also find some of these activities in things that you do for recreation, or with friends and family.

You'll end up with a list of possible opportunities to do the activities that you enjoy. Then you can match them up against the Skill Level and Reward columns on your "Personal Inventory" chart. For each possibility, ask yourself, "Is this something I have the skill to do? If not, should I toss it out or should I look for ways to improve my skills in that area? Or, is this something I'm already skilled at, but I enjoy it so much that I want to get better, now that I have the time?"

Next, ask yourself, "Will this opportunity provide the rewards I'm looking for?" If you're looking for money, and it's a volunteer opportunity, it probably won't. If you like to learn, and it offers a chance for self-improvement, it might fit your needs. Matching skills, enjoyment, and rewards is what you're after.

As a vocational counselor, I've gone through this evaluation process with hundreds of clients over the years. Some were just beginning their careers, some were in the middle but looking for more satisfaction, and some were facing retirement. All found the "Personal Inventory" a valuable process for planning a more useful and rewarding life.

If you think this process has some value for you, but you're having trouble getting enough direction from it, you might consider consulting with a vocational guidance counselor. They can use some test instruments that will help you further identify your interest patterns. Look for a counselor who will use a measurement that compares your interest patterns to various occupations, such as the *Strong-Campbell Interest Inventory*, and a measurement that looks at what your reward needs are, such as the *Minnesota Importance Questionnaire.*

Check with the psychology department of your nearest college or university. They should either have a vocational guidance service, or be able to refer you to an agency or individual in your area. The cost is usually about $250 to administer the tests and hold a couple of interpretive sessions.

Just as the pursuit of new interests doesn't need to wait for retirement, neither does obtaining new rewards. If you have a clear understanding of just what rewards you need for self-fulfillment, it will be easier to find them in your current situation.

Use your "Personal Inventory" as a blueprint. It spells out what you like to do, how well you do it, and what kind of rewards you're looking for. It says "This is me. These are the things I do. These are the things I like to do. I'm good at some of them, I'm working to become better at some others, and I know why I do them." Use this chart to develop a *plan* to find ways in the coming years to identify enjoyable activities, use or improve your skills, and find ways to apply them in areas that will furnish some of your most desired rewards.

7

Opening to a New World

An Action Plan

Up to this point, the purpose of *Closing Doors, Opening Worlds* has been to get you thinking about how the changes in your life are going to affect you. You've read about how similar changes have affected those who have already gone through the retirement process. The problems they encountered should alert you to problems you can expect. Their personal stories about how they successfully resolved some of those problems should suggest some ideas about how you can make the most of your own future. Now it's time for you to start putting some of those ideas into action.

The three princes of Serendip went on a great
journey. They never reached their destination,
but many marvelous things happened along
the way. They were always making discoveries,
by accidents and sagacity, of things they were
not in quest of.

(Old legend from Sri Lanka)

You've probably heard the word *serendipity.* This legend is where it comes from. It means the happy occurrence of things that you weren't really looking for. In order for serendipity to occur, however, a couple of things need to happen. First, you have to have some direction. The three princes of Serendip were going somewhere, they weren't just standing around waiting. Second, you have to be living your life in a way that allows serendipity to happen.

> *When people were leaving the center after completing treatment, I used to hear Wally tell them, "Now go out and let the good things happen to you." I wasn't sure just what he meant by that, and finally I asked him to explain. He said, "It's simple. These people were living their lives in such a way that the good things just couldn't happen. Now that they've got things together and have some direction, you'll be amazed at how the good things seem to just happen."*

(Fifty-five-year-old man)

Many people came back to me over the years and told me how serendipity had worked for them. Sometimes they'd call it luck: "I just can't believe how lucky I've been since retirement. It seems like good things just happen to me." But the ones that it happened to had those two elements in place. They were trying to live their lives according to their value system, and they were trying to improve themselves. If you're working on personal and spiritual growth, and you have direction in your life, serendipity will happen to you, too.

If you've completed your "Personal Inventory," you've been doing a lot of thinking about what you've done with your life, and what you'd like to do with the rest of it. How can you go about turning those thoughts into actions?

Don't try to just drift into it. You may get where you want that way, but it's much more likely to happen if you have a plan, a road map drawn by those who have made the journey before you. And the time to start on the trip is *now*.

Direction

I enjoyed the first couple of years after I retired. I did many of the things I had planned to do, enjoyed my new freedom, and relaxed a lot. It was pleasant, but it wasn't very fulfilling. After a while, I started getting bored and restless. I had a feeling that I wasn't getting enough out of life, or putting enough into it. I felt like I was on the shelf, with the important part of my life far behind me. I didn't like that idea. I still had things to do in this world. Somebody told me that their retirement was going to be the three R's—rest, relaxation, and recreation. Well, for me at least, there has to be a fourth R— relevance. I need to feel like there's a reason for my existence.

(Sixty-six-year-old man)

Many parts of the past have given direction to your life without your having to give much thought to it. Your job probably had monthly, quarterly, or annual goals. If you have children, you most likely had some ideas about how you wanted them to turn out, and what it would take to get them there. Other goals, financial or personal, had some influence on the direction of your life. Now, much of that is gone. What will give direction to the rest of your life?

Purpose, values, needs, and wants are what give direction for most people. Maybe you have a good understanding of those already, and are pretty clear on your direction. Read on anyway. You might find some ways to focus your life that will make your efforts more effective, more enjoyable, or more relevant to your current situation.

> *Yes, I have a purpose in life. It's to profess my faith in the goodness of people, and demonstrate it by the way I live. I believe I have a responsibility to others in doing that. Raising the kids gave me a chance to teach others why I believe what I believe, and hopefully to influence them by my example. My job provided a chance to do that, too. The purpose is still there, and I work towards it, but it's harder to find ways to do it with the job gone and the kids grown.*

(Fifty-eight-year-old woman)

Today Is the First Day of the Rest of Your Life

You've probably heard that one a thousand times, but it's still true and applies to you. If you're going to live differently in the future, today's the day to start.

• Draw a bold circle around today's date on the calendar, and always remember it as the day you started.

Have a System to Keep You On the Path

• Start keeping a journal today.

Unless you're more self-disciplined than 99% of the people in this world, you'll need something to keep you focused on this journey. The advantage of a journal is that you can use it to look back and confirm that you're headed in the right direction, or analyze how you strayed off the path. It doesn't have to be elaborate, but be sure to make an entry *every day,* even if it's only, "I didn't do anything today to advance towards my goals." A good entry for today would be, "Today I started the journey to get what I want out of the rest of my life. I promise to make a note in this journal every day so that I can keep track of how I'm doing."

• Start to work today towards your goals; don't wait for them to come to you.

> *Ed was at the doctor's office to get the report on his annual physical. "How'm I doing, Doc?,"*
> *he asked. "How long do you think I'll live?"*
> *"Well," said the doctor, "we can never predict that exactly, you know."*
> *"Can't you at least give me an opinion?" said Ed.*
> *"If I were you, Ed," said the doctor, "I wouldn't buy any green bananas."*

Too many people go through life waiting for something to happen. "I'll get to that in a few days," we tell ourselves. Or, "One of these days I'm going to get started on that. It's something I've always wanted to do, and one of these days I'm going to." It's like buying green bananas. You can't eat them now, but one of these days.... The problem is, you might not be around when they get ripe.

A friend of mine gave me a round lapel pin that had the word "tuit" printed on it. "What's this?" I asked him. "Well," he said, "you're always saying that you're going to write a book when you get 'a round tuit.' Now you've got one, so get on with it."

Examining your past to better understand yourself has been a useful exercise, but it's action that will determine what the rest of your life is going to be. Get "a round tuit" today.

Don't Be a Victim of Your Past;
Be the Creator of Your Future

- Keep looking forward, not back.

  I spent a lot of my life feeling sorry for myself or beating myself up emotionally. I came from a very poor family and didn't have some of the opportunities that most people have. I didn't get much of an education because I thought I couldn't afford to go to college. Then later on in life, I looked back and realized that I probably could have gotten that education if I'd made the effort. I blamed myself for that, and I spent so much time worrying about what I could or should have done differently in the past, that I never got any satisfaction from what I was doing in the present. I did fairly well in spite of that, though, and when I was forced to retire at sixty, I knew I had the chance to do some of the things I wanted.

  A counselor helped me learn to spend my energy just trying to do the best I can each day, and stop regretting the past or worrying about the future. When I live that way, I usually feel good about what I've accomplished that day. And you know what? Those good days have just piled up one at a time until the bad days are so far away that I don't regret them anymore.

  (Sixty-two-year-old man)

- Promise yourself that you will do at least one thing every day for self-improvement or advancement towards your goals. Log it in your journal to keep tabs on yourself.

  If there is anything you can do about things that you

regret from your past, take action now, and get on with your life. Don't waste energy regretting things you *didn't* do. Instead, focus on accomplishing something worthwhile today. The way to create the future that you want is to do something today that will contribute to those goals.

Don't spend much time dwelling on old accomplishments either. It's OK to be proud of what you've done in the past, but it's not going to do much for today or for your future. Don't be like the old man who spent so much time talking about what he had done in the past that he finally grew as bored as his listeners—and died.

Expectations

In youth we overestimate our potential, in age we underestimate ourselves.

• Set high expectations for yourself as to what you can accomplish in the way of growth or self-fulfillment each day.

This is not a job, where if you don't meet the goals you might be fired. Self-improvement and enjoyment are what will make you feel good about yourself at the end of the day. If you make even a small step towards your goal, that's worthwhile. If you set your expectations too low, you'll just cheat yourself.

Attitudes

• Don't be judgmental of others; show respect and an open mind. You will learn more that way, and your attitude will be reflected back to you.

When you retire, you won't have the forced contact with others that you had on the job, so there's always a danger of isolation. Behavior that invites open, respectful relationships will increase your potential for being involved in healthy, genuine friendships as you move into your later years. Show the same respect for yourself. Expect the best, and the best is more likely to happen to you. If you convey an attitude that you expect others to treat you with interest, respect, and affection, that's the way people will respond to you. Remember, people will behave like you expect them to behave.

Structure and Discipline

No matter how sincere your intention to make the most of your opportunities, it's easy to drift off the path without the schedules and deadlines you had on the job. Find some ways to keep at least some structure in your life.

• Set short-term goals and give yourself a reasonable deadline to meet them. Enjoy your flexibility, but schedule at least a few activities every week to ensure that you are keeping some structure and balance in your life. Enter your goals, deadlines, and schedule in your journal so that you can check up on yourself.

Predictors of Success

In Chapter 1, I listed ten characteristics that seemed to predict success in retirement. The happiest and most successful people shared most, or all, of these characteristics. As you prepare your plan for the future, measure your strengths and weaknesses against this list. What strengths can you capitalize on, and which do you need to improve if you're going to be successful?

(1) **They had a realistic idea of their strengths and weaknesses.** If you've examined your personal and spiritual identity, you should have a good idea of what strengths

and weaknesses of character you bring to your commitment to values. If you're still not sure, have a talk with your spiritual advisor, or a friend in whom you have trust and confidence. Ask them to give you a frank and honest evaluation of what your strengths and weaknesses are. We often need feedback from others to see ourselves as we really are.

You also need to assess the skills you will use to pursue activities that fulfill those values. Go back to the chart you made in Chapter 6, the one titled "Personal Inventory." You evaluated your skill level at performing certain activities that you said you liked, the activities that brought you the kind of rewards you wanted out of life. Do you think you made an accurate assessment? Once again, if you're not sure, it might be useful to get someone else's opinion.

• Now make a list of your spiritual and personal strengths and weaknesses, and of the skills you will need to fulfill your goals. Decide which are the most important, and which you want to improve. Choose at least one personal weakness, or skill that needs to be developed, and start working on it today.

(2) **They set high standards for themselves. They measured their progress against their own standards rather than the opinions of others.** Look at the goals that you've set for yourself. What is going to be acceptable to you as far as attainment of, or progress toward, those goals? Those are your standards.

• In your own words, write down why those standards are acceptable to you. If you can explain it, then you will know whether you're setting your own standards or are influenced by what others might think.

(3) **Their identity was not tied to their job, but rather to**

their spiritual beliefs and moral values. Most had an active religious affiliation. If much of your identity in the past has come from your job, you need to look for off-the-job activities that will involve your beliefs and values. If that's where your identity already lies, take advantage of opportunities to strengthen it.

• Exercising and exploring your beliefs and values will strengthen your feelings of identity. If you have a religious affiliation, participate in both study and practice. If you don't have a religious affiliation, search for a church that meets your needs. If you do not choose to belong to a church, continue to explore your own spirituality through study, reading, personal rituals, or discussion.

(4) **Throughout life they tried to devote time and effort to improving themselves.** Whether it's improving your tennis game, learning a new language, mastering a home computer or having a friend teach you how to cook goulash, life is more interesting and rewarding when you can feel that somehow you're better than you were yesterday. During retirement, you'll have more time and opportunity to improve yourself than you've had in the past. Take advantage of it.

Self-improvement can be as formal as starting a course of study that will lead to a certificate or degree. It can be as informal as reading a couple of pages in a thought-provoking book. Give yourself credit for even the smallest steps, and don't shy away from more grandiose efforts because of fear of failure. Remember, you're the one who's setting the standards. You can decide what degree of progress is considered success.

• Make a promise to yourself that, starting now, you will do one thing each day to improve yourself. Each day, whatever that improvement was, write it down in your journal. Set a time, either at the beginning or end of your week, that you will review your journal to check your progress.

(5) **They were involved in leisure, social, and volunteer activities during employment; their job was not their whole life.** Maybe your life is already full of activities that are apart from the job. Be sure, though, that they're filling your needs—that they are activities that you truly enjoy, or that satisfy your values. Go back to your "Personal Inventory" chart from Chapter 6 again, and check your activities against the list of 1s and 2s, the things that you said you enjoyed the most. If you aren't currently involved doing at least several of those enjoyable activities, it's time to find some new projects that will include them.

• Set a goal for yourself that you will find at least one new leisure, social, or volunteer activity that would earn a 1 or 2 on your "Personal Inventory" chart. Give yourself a deadline, and enter it in your journal.

(6) **They were team players. They liked working with others towards a common goal.** You may be a person who enjoys working alone, or believe that you are more effective that way. Most likely, however, your job involved some kind of team effort, and you'll be missing that. Socializing may provide the contact with others that you need, but it usually doesn't create the "team spirit" that exists when a group of people are working together towards a goal they consider worthwhile.

• Be sure you're involved in at least one activity, whether it be in your avocation, or with a church, community, recreational, volunteer or education group, that will join you with others, working together to accomplish something worthwhile.

(7) **They were able to define their interests and what they wanted out of life.** If you put some effort into your "Personal Inventory" chart in Chapter 6, you should have a good picture of where you are on this issue right now. But through your new activities and acquaintances, you might discover interests that you never knew you had. That's one of the exciting things about personal growth. It's serendipity in action, and, life might open up a whole new world of opportunity for you.

• Keep examining your interests and search for ways to develop and practice new ones. Go back to your "Personal Inventory" chart at least once a month and add any new activities that you have found interesting.

(8) **They enjoyed using their skills in service to others.** One of the best ways to feel useful, worthwhile, and good about yourself is to do something that improves the well-being of others. It can be as simple as calling someone who is lonely, giving a compliment to someone who is down, or as grand as leading an organization to feed the world's poor. The reward comes from the act of giving, not from the scope of the project.

• Each day, do at least one thing, no matter how small, that is a service to someone else. If you aren't comfortable with direct service, be a "behind the scenes" person in some project that contributes to the welfare of others.

(9) **Though not wealthy, they were relatively stable financially; there was balance between their income and their lifestyle.** There seems to be no correlation between wealth and happiness, and there is certainly none between wealth and worthiness. Money may make life easier, but not more rewarding. Even so, financial worries can inhibit your ability to get on with your personal growth.

• If you have financial concerns or problems, get some expert advice. All large cities and most smaller ones have counseling available at little or no cost. Check with your local United Way, Credit Bureau, or Senior Citizen Center.

(10) **They learned to become flexible. They anticipated and planned for changes in their lives.** Sorry, the changes in your life won't come to an end when you retire. They'll keep coming the rest of your life. The good news is that if you've worked through the processes of anticipating and preparing for change that are outlined in this book, you should have more skills for dealing with change than most people ever develop.

• Remember, anticipating and preparing for change is a life-long process. Periodically, go through your journal. Look at the changes that developed in the last several months and note how you handled them. Learn from your own experiences. Then try to project any changes in relationships, lifestyle, or structure that are likely to occur in the coming months, and develop a plan to prepare for them.

These are the attributes of people who have been most successful and happy in retirement. It may look like an overwhelming list of things to do, but you already have some of these attributes, and working on the others can be an interesting and enjoyable challenge. You might not achieve all of them, but progress is what's important.

Balance

• Remember, whatever your activities, to keep some balance in your life. Every week should include activities that involve physical exercise, mental stimulation, productive work, recreation, spiritual exercise, leisure, socializing with others, and spending time with friends and family.

Weekly Scorecard

Just to get your action plan started, try keeping score for yourself a week at a time to be sure that you're including the activities you will need to help keep you headed in the right direction.

• List at least one activity that you were involved in this week for each category. If you missed any this week, set a goal for that category for the following week.

Photocopy this scorecard and keep it with your other "Personal Inventory" items.

Physical exercise

Mental stimulation

Leisure activity

Spiritual exercise

Self-improvement

Doing something in service to others

Doing something with others

Working towards one of your goals

Entering progress in your journal

8

Dangers Along the Way

Avoiding the Pitfalls

Many people who had a lot of good things going for them as they moved into their later years, got sidetracked and didn't find the happiness they deserved. Fortunately, many found their way back, and you can learn from their experience. There are at least four traps you need to look out for. They are procrastination, isolation, imbalance, and alcohol or other drugs.

Procrastination

When I first retired, I'd sleep till 11:00 A.M.
and then get up and do nothing all day. Now,
I get up at 8:00 A.M. and do nothing all day. See,
I'm working harder at it!

(Eighty-four-year-old man)

Some people are natural self-starters, but many others need a push to get going. Jobs make demands that don't allow people to postpone things. Some thrive under the pressure of deadlines, but left to their own accord, they tend to procrastinate. Putting things off at this stage means that you're delaying making the most of the rest of your life.

If you're one who needed deadlines to get you moving, you're at risk in retirement. If you don't get started doing the things that you want to do with your life, you might not be unhappy—but you won't be as happy as you could be, because you'll miss some opportunities.

> *As I look back, it's not the things I did wrong that I regret. Everybody makes mistakes, and I did what I could to make up for mine. It's the things I didn't do that make me sad. There's no way of making up for those.*
>
> (Seventy-four-year-old woman)

If you're not a self-starter, look for ways to bring some discipline into your life. Make a list of things you want to do, then set deadlines. Keep a journal of your activities, and give yourself a score for how well you're meeting your objectives. Don't spend your life in the *expectation* of living. Get on with it now.

Isolation

> *I've never been a very gregarious person. I didn't seem to need to have other people around me, and I enjoyed being alone, so I thought I wouldn't miss the contact with others that I had at work. And at first I didn't, but after a few months I started to get depressed. I didn't identify it as loneliness; in fact, I didn't even want to be around people. I just felt sad and sorry for myself and kind of lost.*
>
> *The volunteer organization at work kept after me to do some work for them and I finally forced myself to do it. It only took about three*

*days before I was feeling like my old self. I
learned that even though I'm kind of a loner, I
need to be with people at least some of the time.*

(Sixty-two-year-old woman)

Solitude is being alone with yourself by choice, and enjoying it. It gives you a chance to think and reflect, an opportunity to know yourself better. It can be emotionally and spiritually healthy and contribute to your satisfaction with life. But you also need contact with other people. They're like a mirror that reflects your self-image back to you. That reflection is an affirmation of your worth as an individual. *Isolation* is being removed from that contact with others. Without the mirror, you tend to focus on yourself and bring on loneliness and self-pity.

Your job probably forced you to have contact with others, even if you didn't seek it. If you're not naturally outgoing, you may have to find other ways to force that contact. Volunteer work, church activities, recreational programs, membership in groups, or taking classes are some ways of maintaining contact with others. You can use a weekly schedule of activities or your journal to maintain some discipline so that you don't fall into the trap of isolation.

Imbalance

You should use your leisure time to do the things you've always wanted to do. You've earned it. But all play and no work, as they say, will make you a dull person. At any age, you still need balance in your life. The same kind of balance is not necessary for everyone, so you'll have to find out the mix of activities that is best for you. Be sure, however, that your activities include play, productive work, and intellectual and spiritual self-improvement.

> *I've always loved golf, and never had enough time to play—until I retired. Then I golfed every day. Sometimes I'd play eighteen holes in the morning and then watch golf on TV in the afternoon. I knew I was in trouble when my wife started to yell "Fore!" at the dinner table to get my attention.*

(Fifty-eight-year-old man)

Go back to your "Personal Inventory" chart you constructed for Chapter 6. Look at the activities you said were important to you and the rewards you got from them. It's likely that at least some of them fell into categories other than recreation. If you think your life is getting a little lopsided, use that list as a way of getting back on track.

Alcohol and Other Drugs

"I can probably skip this part," you might be saying to yourself right now. "I've never had a problem, and I'm sure not going to start now. Besides, I've already heard so much about that stuff, that I know everything I need to know."

Don't get nervous. I'm not going to tell you to stop drinking. But a lot of things are changing in your life, and they will have an impact on the way you can, or should, change your drinking habits. You need to learn about them to be sure that your use of alcohol doesn't ruin your opportunity for a healthy and happy future.

Throughout this book you've been thinking about the changes that are going to be taking place in your life. Your susceptibility to alcohol is going to change, too. Statistically, your risk of developing a problem with alcohol or other drugs will almost triple over the next ten to fifteen years. Even if you're fortunate and don't develop a problem yourself, the chances are nearly 100% that someone very close to you, a friend or family member, will. So it's worth the effort to be sure you understand just why the risk of substance abuse becomes greater in retirement and later life.

When I ran an alcohol treatment program twenty-five years ago, I always felt that some of the saddest cases were people who developed the disease late in life. "I was a social drinker all my life," they'd say. "I never had any trouble. I was responsible, held a good job, and took care of my family. All of a sudden, I was in a hell of a mess. It happened before I knew what was going on. I'm scared—and I'm ashamed."

Later, as an employee counselor in a large corporation, I began to hear the same story from people I had known for ten years or longer. I knew they were telling the truth when they said they never had a problem during their working years, but they'd be in my office a year after retirement, in tears. "I don't know what happened. This isn't me. I've never been like this. These were going to be my happiest years, and I'm a mess!" They felt ashamed, baffled, and betrayed by their own bodies. It got to a point where I was telling management that if we retired someone with even a hint of a drinking problem, their retirement could be a death sentence.

Why does it happen? Let's review the basics. First, you'll notice that I used the term "alcohol and other drugs." That always confuses some folks who say "I never use drugs, so none of this applies to me." It's extremely important to understand that illegal street drugs, alcohol, and prescription mood-altering drugs are all pretty much the same when it comes to their potential for abuse and addiction.

That potential is multiplied when they are used together, as frequently happens when a social drinker begins taking prescription medication. You may have never used a street drug in your life, but if you are a casual drinker and have just been put on medication by your doctor, you have greatly increased your risk potential.

Just when can you say that it's actually a problem? There are many labels and definitions out there, and most of them turn people off and raise their defenses. So let's try to define it in a behavioral sense. The one I've found most useful and least threatening is this: *If you use alcohol, prescription drugs, or street drugs, and that use interferes with any important area of your life—your health, your finances, your relationship with other people, or your self-respect, and you keep on using—you are chemically dependent. You don't keep on using something that harms these important areas unless you are dependent upon it. This is harmful dependence. It's a permanent, progressive, and terminal disease.*

You'll notice that this definition doesn't say anything about how much or how often you drink. I've known people who have used alcohol every day for many years, and never let it interfere with their lives. I've also known people who only drink a couple of times a year, but when they do, it causes problems. So throw out your ideas about quantity or frequency. The important issue is whether or not it causes any trouble in your life.

Why does chemical dependency develop in some people and not others? There are three factors that need to be present before someone develops this condition.

The first factor is *physical predisposition*. In many ways, harmful dependence is a physical disease. Your body actually reacts to mood-changing chemicals in a way that is different from people who don't have this physical predisposition. This factor is being increasingly substantiated by medical and genetic studies. There's also a strong hereditary factor, especially as it pertains to alcohol. So even though you're a "normal" drinker yourself, if you have close blood relatives who have had problems with alcohol, be aware that you are at high risk. If you have this physical factor, you're not going to be able to use alcohol safely. How self-controlled you are has nothing to do with it. Understanding this physical and genetic factor usually makes it easier for people to accept that they are at high risk. It takes away some of the old stereotypes about "weak character."

Then there is a *psychological factor*. Certain personality types seem more prone to the disease: perfectionists; people with strict moral standards, who are self-critical and set high standards for themselves; and people who were raised in authoritarian settings. Some of my own research showed a correlation between harmful dependence and intelligence and education. The smarter you are, the more you're at risk. And finally, as people deal with change in their lives, some are more prone to turn to chemicals to alleviate the discomfort of emotional stress.

The third factor is *exposure*. You might have the physical predisposition and the emotional makeup, but you won't develop a problem if you don't use mood-changing chemicals.

Now let's take a look at how these three factors may increase your susceptibility to harmful dependence as you go through the physical and emotional changes that are likely to take place in the next several years.

The physical factor. You may not have inherited a

tendency towards addiction, and you may have been drinking socially without harm for many years. As you age, however, your body changes, and different organs change their functions at different rates. You may have noticed some of these changes already.

Even though you're in excellent health and are taking care of yourself, you may find that you don't tolerate certain foods the way you used to. That's a sign of those internal changes. It doesn't cause a problem as long as you're willing to change some of your eating habits. You may have noticed that it's not as easy to lose weight as it used to be. The same combination of diet and exercise that you used to shed five pounds in a week when you were thirty, may only get rid of one pound when you're forty. That's because your body is metabolizing food differently than it did when you were thirty. It shouldn't be a surprise that your body also handles alcohol differently as you age. Most people, for example, find that it takes less alcohol to achieve the same feeling that a greater amount caused when they were younger.

Changes in diet or physical activity can exacerbate the change in the ability of your body to handle alcohol, too. You can't count on the physical factors to remain constant. Your body may have been able to handle alcohol for years without a problem, but perhaps it can't now, or won't be able to sometime in the future. Be on the lookout for these changes!

As you grow older, there's an increasing likelihood that you'll be using various forms of medication, both prescribed and over-the-counter. Many of these medications can greatly change the ability of your body to tolerate alcohol. Alcohol alone may not cause any problems, and neither would the medication by itself. But put the two together and sometimes it can produce what is called *potentiation,* or a multiplied effect. It's like adding 2 and 2 and coming up with 97.

The psychological factor. You've been a well-adjusted person all these years, and you still may be, but you're dealing with profound changes in your life. Your support systems will be different, your relationships are changing. Your daily activities are different, and you're looking for different ways to find satisfaction in life. In other words, you're now pouring that alcohol on a psyche that, no matter how healthy, is different than the one that you used to pour it on. You have no way of predicting what the interaction is going to be.

You'll also lose some of the reference points that helped you judge your own behavior. During your work life there were many checks and balances. You had to follow a schedule, and if you didn't, you knew it or someone would call your attention to it. There were various ways that your job could be measured, and so you generally knew whether or not you were performing well. You might be irritable and crabby for days without realizing it yourself, but someone would eventually confront you about it. In retirement, many of those controls will be gone, so your drinking could be affecting you negatively without your really being aware of it.

The exposure factor. Perhaps most important is the last factor. During your years on the job, there were many things that controlled your opportunity to drink. In most companies having a drink with lunch is not acceptable. You'd work late, come home, and have a drink before dinner. Then you'd have things to do and likely wouldn't have another drink. You had to retire early so you'd be ready to work the next morning. Now things have changed and most of those constraints have disappeared. What's to keep you from drinking whenever and wherever you want to?

It Could Happen to You

I had known Janet for nearly twenty years. She had spent her entire career in a medium-sized company, advancing to the position of comptroller. She was a major contributor to the growth and success of the company. In another era she probably would have been president of the company, but her career had developed when that was just about out of the question for a woman. She was liked and respected by her colleagues. She was one of the most organized, disciplined, and self-controlled people I have ever known. Then Janet took early retirement. A year later, she was sitting in my office, and she was falling apart.

"Talking about this is the most difficult thing I've ever had to do," she finally blurted out. I waited. "I can't control my drinking!" She went on to give me her drinking history, much of which I already knew. For most of the last thirty years she had been a regular, moderately heavy drinker. She'd have one cocktail nearly every night, sometimes two, and occasionally three at a party or special event.

She never let herself cross the line. To see Janet drunk would have been such a shock to anyone who knew her that they wouldn't have believed it if they saw it. And that image, the pride in her own self-discipline, was enough motivation to keep Janet in control. In addition, her pride in her work was such that she would have worried about a hangover affecting her efficiency. She never let her drinking get out of hand.

Janet probably had the first problem factor, a physical predisposition—there was alcoholism in her hereditary background. She certainly had many of the characteristics of the psychological factor—perfectionism, high standards, and intelligence. But her self-control, and all the constraints she placed on herself in order to be so effective on her job, limited the third problem factor, exposure.

"When I first retired," she said, "I didn't change my drinking pattern. I'd usually have a cocktail before dinner and that was it. After a couple of months, that changed without my realizing it, but only gradually at first. I live alone, you know, and on nights when I was home I'd start reading or get engrossed in a TV show, and I'd find myself fixing myself a second one, and sometimes a third. Why not? There didn't seem to be any harm in it. If once in a while I had a little too much to drink, there was no problem. I knew I didn't have to get up early and face a demanding job.

"Somewhere along the way I started to occasionally have a drink with lunch. Usually I did this when I was alone but sometimes I'd have one if I met friends at a restaurant. Maybe I'd have a glass of wine. This was something I'd never done before, but it certainly isn't out of the ordinary. But now I was not only drinking more, I was spreading it out over the day. If my "happy hour" cocktail turned into two or three, I might never get around to having dinner.

"Well, I'm really ashamed to admit this, but I convinced myself there wasn't really anything wrong with having a drink instead of my usual cup of coffee in the morning while I was reading the paper. I was drinking all day long, and I was able to convince myself that it was normal!

"Last week I went in for my annual physical. When my

doctor called me in to discuss the results, he started asking me all kinds of questions about my drinking. I was pretty defensive at first, but when he told me I was beginning to show signs of liver damage, I finally admitted to him, and to myself, just how much I had been drinking. He told me that I needed to quit completely. I didn't like to hear that, but I knew he was right. I'd likely cause serious damage if I continued, so I decided to quit. I didn't want to, but I thought it would be easy. I've always been able to do anything I set my mind to do.

"I paced the floor for three days. I couldn't sleep, couldn't think, and I felt extremely depressed. I finally decided that what I needed to do was taper off. I went to the liquor store and bought a pint instead of my usual liter, because I was serious about this tapering-off bit. I drank the whole pint within two hours after I got home. That was more than I have ever had at one sitting in my whole life. I was drunk. And this morning I feel worse than ever. I can't quit! I've never felt so helpless in my life."

I arranged for Janet's doctor to give her some withdrawal medication and sent her to be evaluated for an outpatient treatment program, which she entered voluntarily the following day. She applied her usual self-discipline and diligence to the treatment process and hasn't had a drink in the ten years since then. Janet had a successful recovery, but this is an unusually strong person, and she got help before her condition had deteriorated too far, either mentally or physically. If it hadn't been for a fortuitous and prudent intervention by her doctor, she might have been dead within a year.

What does Janet's story mean for you? You should assess both your current drinking status and your risk potential.

Because part of the process of becoming chemically dependent is to delude yourself that it isn't happening, I encourage you to invite someone who is close to you to help you in this self-assessment process.

Start with the *predisposition* factor. In the general population, the predisposition risk runs about eight to ten percent. If you have close blood relatives (a father, mother, uncle, aunt, brother, or sister) who have exhibited alcohol problems, the risk is closer to twenty percent. If the problem is on both sides of the family, the risk increases greatly.

Next, take a look at whether anything has changed about your drinking in the last several years. Are you drinking more? More frequently? Does alcohol seem to affect you differently than it used to? Any change can be a warning sign. If it seems to take more to achieve a certain feeling than it used to, you may be building tolerance—a serious warning sign. If it takes significantly less, it could be a sign of liver damage, and you should consult your physician.

If anything about your physical status has changed, such as a weight gain or loss, change in diet, change in exercise habits, or newly-developed physical problems such as heart disease or high blood pressure, you should also reassess your drinking habits. You can't rely on your body to handle alcohol the way it did prior to these physical changes. If you're using any prescribed or over-the-counter medication, insist on a full explanation and recommendation from your physician about any possible interactions with alcohol.

The second factor, *psychological,* is harder to define and to apply to yourself. Again, it's important to have the input of someone who knows you well. Start by facing the fact that you will be going through some strong emotional changes when you retire. If you're working on many of the positive restructuring projects that are discussed in this book, and things are progressing well, you're probably doing OK. But if you're finding yourself depressed, or anxious about the changes that are taking place in your life, be careful. Healthy drinkers, when they are faced with these kinds of difficulties, drink *less* than usual, to be sure that they have all their mental resources to deal with the problem at hand. If you find that you're using alcohol to help yourself relax or feel more confident as you go through this process, you're headed for trouble.

Ask yourself if drinking seems to be very important to you. If it's just a social beverage, it won't be. If, however, you find yourself being concerned about the opportunity to follow your drinking ritual, or if you get upset when something interferes with it, that's another very strong warning sign.

If anyone had told me that alcohol was too important to me, I would have been offended. I was a social drinker. Alcohol was a social drink. There's nothing harmful in that. Then I went on a fishing trip with four of my friends. We spent a whole week at a remote lake in Canada. We were flown in and left there with provisions, bait, and everything we needed for the week. Jack was supposed to bring the booze. It wasn't till we were unpacking after the plane had left that we discovered Jack had forgotten it. I was ready to kill him. I couldn't understand why everyone else could just laugh it off. I was angry for the whole week and I let everyone

> *know it. I didn't really forgive Jack for being so*
> *stupid till two years later, when I was in treat-*
> *ment for my drinking problem.*
>
> (Forty-seven-year-old man)

The *exposure* factor is a little easier to deal with. Although the previous paragraphs might sound like you'll never drink again, this one should be more reassuring. The bottom line is, if you have a drinking pattern now that hasn't caused you any trouble, you probably don't need to change it, although you should be alert to all the warnings. You can drink less, of course, but whatever you do, don't drink more. Especially, don't drink *more frequently!* One of the key factors in physical addiction is the amount of time that the body's cells are exposed to the chemical. Adding daytime drinking to a previous pattern of a drink or two at night multiplies your dependency risk many times.

Finally, learn as much as you can about chemical dependency. No matter how healthy you are mentally and physically, your risk factor in later life is probably above twenty percent. If you were at this level of risk for any other serious disease, you'd want to know all about it. You should do the same for chemical dependency.

You've earned your retirement, and if you've been working on the issues that have been raised in this book, you probably have a good start on the road to a rewarding and fulfilling future. Be sure you don't let an unexpected pitfall like procrastination, isolation, or harmful dependence derail you. Now that you're forewarned, a review of your journal can tell you whether you might be drifting towards danger, and the action plan from Chapter 7 suggests several ways to help you get back on track.

9

Managing Employee Retirement for Fun and Profit

What Business Can Do

Business has a responsibility to help employees plan and prepare for retirement. If you're an employer, meeting that responsibility can be one of the best investments you ever make. It will pay off in improved productivity, loyalty, and morale.

Prior to the industrial revolution of the last century, work was largely an individual or family affair. Artisans, shopkeepers, or farmers worked alone or in family units. A person's sense of identity and belonging, the sharing of values and purpose, came from an association with the community, the extended family, and the church.

As industry changed, it brought people together to work in larger groups. People began to draw some of their sense of community from the workplace. As the workplace became an important source of identity, it was a natural progression to identify with co-workers, business owners, or the industry at large in establishing a sense of values and purpose.

As a result of these changes, many social scientists today believe that the workplace has largely replaced church, community, and even family as a primary source for identity and self-worth. Arguments can be made as to whether or not this is a healthy development, but it's a reality nonetheless. In accepting some of the benefits, like greater loyalty and dedication from employees, business must in turn accept some responsibility towards them.

What can an employer do to help their workers prepare for the emotional changes brought about by retirement, cutbacks, layoffs, or other life changes? There are many things you can do throughout the career cycle that will help your employees prepare for these changes, and make them healthier, happier, and more effective workers in the process.

Attitude

Over the last several decades, Asian companies have gained a reputation for achieving business success by winning genuine commitment from their employees. They did this by exercising and demonstrating a fundamental belief—that each person is an equally important part of the organization and could be trusted to give his/her best effort. In recent years, Western companies have tried to duplicate that success through a series of fads and buzzwords—employee involvement, quality circles and the latest, empowerment. Some have successfully integrated the idea of equal worth into their management philosophy and enjoy improved morale and productivity as a result. Many others, though, have introduced the form and process of these ideas without the substance—a basic belief in the inherent worth of each person.

The heart of a good company is a genuine respect for the dignity of every worker. If you have that, and can demonstrate it, you'll be rewarded by employee loyalty and respect in return. This kind of mutual respect not only makes the job more pleasant and meaningful, but contributes to efficiency. It's much easier for employees to accept changes and criticism, for example, if they know they're respected. A reorganization that results in some demotions is seen as a group effort rather than a personal affront. People who have been promoted beyond their ability can be moved back instead of the dehumanizing and inefficient system of "up or out." Workers also will feel free to make rational decisions about when to retire, instead of being forced out or leaving the job in frustration.

Education

Many companies provide tuition reimbursement or other plans that encourage employees to improve their skills. Some even provide education on the job site. Often, though, these opportunities are only offered to people in certain job categories, and the education is strictly job-related. Try to find ways to broaden learning opportunities for all workers. You'll be rewarded with employees who are not only grateful, but more efficient and creative.

You probably have employees who have expertise in areas that might not seem directly related to your business, but would be something that other employees would find to be of interest. Why not ask those experts if they'd volunteer to share their expertise with others through seminars at lunch or after work? All you'd have to do is provide the forum and the facilities. I bet they'd jump at the chance. Wider education will broaden the skills of your employees, and that will prepare them to select more appropriate career options within the company. That's good for them, and for the business. It will also provide them with a wider range of interests and opportunities to pursue in retirement. You'll have happier and healthier employees, and happier and healthier retirees.

Participation

One of the rewards of working for an organization is that it helps answer an important human need, a need to be a part of something worthwhile, working for a larger purpose. Be sure that your employees at every level understand the purpose of your business. Try to find ways to give them an opportunity to have some input into defining what that purpose is. It will give them a feeling of worth and importance now, and they'll be able to approach retirement with greater satisfaction and dignity, because they'll feel that their work was involved in doing something that was worth doing.

If your company donates money to community projects, try doing it in a way that will give all employees an opportunity to participate. You might even involve them in the process of selecting which projects to support. This gives them a sense of participation and pride in the company, and it also begins an involvement with the community that can continue after retirement. Here's how it worked for one large company with many small locations throughout the United States:

> *About fifteen years ago we began to question whether our corporate philanthropy was really accomplishing as much as it could. We were primarily involved in large projects, and they were usually national in scope. We decided to ask our employees how they felt about the way we were spending those charitable dollars, and we learned a few things. First, we*

found that most of our employees weren't even aware of our philanthropy. Most of the projects were too remote, or involved support from a lot of donors, so our company name didn't get much attention. Second, and I think more important, our employees didn't see that our efforts had any impact on their own community. Even if they were aware of what we were doing, it didn't mean much to them individually; it was impersonal as far as they were concerned.

We held group meetings at some of our smaller locations and asked employees to identify projects in their own communities that deserved support. At nearly every location, there were one or more worthwhile opportunities for us to make an important contribution.

We decided to try three locations that first year, as an experiment. It was more successful than we ever could have imagined, because some things happened that we didn't expect. Our employees were enthusiastic because they were their *projects, and so they donated a lot of their own time and expertise to see that they were done right. We were recognized as an important part of the community because both the financial and the personal contributions were seen as good citizenship. We don't try to use our philanthropy as a way of buying publicity, but it's sure nice when you get some good press and can feel that you've earned it.*

But the nicest surprise of all was the effect it had on our employees. You could see that they were proud of themselves, and proud of the company. Morale was at an all-time high. Involving them in this whole process multiplied the positive effect of our donation many, many times. Now we do all our corporate giving this way—we do it at the local level and involve our people in both the selection and implementation of the projects. I can't think of anything in the last fifteen years that has had such a positive impact on our organization.

(Vice-president, Community Relations)

Career Planning

Career planning isn't just for employees who are on the management track; it's for everybody at every level of your organization. One way of showing respect for employees is to demonstrate a genuine interest in their career aspirations. Performance reviews should always include some serious discussion of the employee's goals for advancement, or their interest in changing duties. It's an opportunity to find out more about what skills they have now, or will need to develop in order to become more productive.

This needs to be a two-way process—the employee should have a chance to explore possible opportunities, and the reviewer should be able to suggest strategies for ways to gain new skills. The concept of career planning for employees at all levels of your organization will improve the caliber of your work force now, and will have a positive impact on their future—they will develop new skills and interests that can be used to make retirement more interesting and rewarding.

Discuss future retirement plans with each employee during these performance reviews, starting many years before the due date. It may influence their career choices during the last years of work. It will be much easier to do realistic succession planning if you have a clear idea of what each employee is considering. Both you and the employee can make more rational, informed decisions about retirement if it's been a part of the performance discussions for years.

Get Some Extra Dividends

You've invested a lot in your employees over the years, and you can still get some dividends after they've retired. Many companies maintain a cadre of "permanent, part-time employees" who are on call to come in and help out on special projects, or when the work load is heavy. If you use retirees for this purpose you'll have a dependable pool of employees with proven skills who know how the company operates, and who are likely to be more dedicated than outsiders. Such a program also provides an opportunity for retirees to maintain old contacts and old feelings of belonging to the work group. They can also earn a few extra bucks in the process.

Helping Employees Support Community Service

A formal retiree volunteer organization, sponsored and supported by the company, can be an effective way to match the energy and expertise of your retired employees to the needs that exist in your community. At low cost, you can provide office space, telephones, and other equipment to support volunteerism and other community service activities. It's a way to encourage retirees to remain active in useful and fulfilling activities, it's socially responsible, and it enhances your corporate image in the community while increasing the impact of your philanthropy. Here's one retiree's opinion:

> *Because our volunteer organization is able to identify and prioritize the needs, I believe I'm able to use my skills much more effectively than if I just went out looking for volunteer opportunities on my own. I also feel like I'm a part of the company, in a way that's different than before I retired. I always felt OK about the company, but now when I can see first-hand what we're accomplishing in the community, I feel some real pride in being identified with the company name!*

They're Still Part of the Family

Everyone has a need to belong, and feeling that you're still part of the company even after retirement can help fill that need. Look for ways to include retirees in company functions like annual parties, or through communications like company newsletters. This helps retirees maintain a sense of pride and identity with the company, and they will feel that their years of effort were worthwhile. It also sends a message to current employees that when they're gone, they won't be forgotten.

Formalize Retirement

Even though you might find ways for retirees to continue to participate in company affairs through part-time work, retiree groups, volunteer activities, or company functions, it's important that both the company and the retiree recognize that they're entering a different stage of the relationship. Retirement parties, awards, speeches, and special announcements are all ways to formalize that change. These can be ways of honoring the employee for service, and at the same time acknowledge that the employer/employee relationship has entered a new stage. This helps the employee make an easier emotional adjustment to the change.

Retirement-Planning Seminars

You'll be doing your employees a big favor if you start to educate them about retirement options years before they retire. They'll be better prepared emotionally and financially, and there will be a payoff for the company if employees are better able to make informed choices about retirement.

Companies that offer these programs usually invite employees and their partners to a seminar about five years before the earliest likely retirement date. Typically, four seminars are presented. One will explore alternative living options such as retirement communities, another will deal with financial planning, a third will discuss health issues, and one will address emotional adjustments to retirement and aging.

You should be able to find resources in your community to address each of these issues. The cost is usually minimal. If you're a small employer, consider banding together with other companies to provide these seminars. They'll help give direction to your employees at this important time in their lives.

10

Approaching Autumn

For a More Fulfilling Life

Some seem never to grow old. Always active in thought, always ready to adapt to new ideas. Satisfied, yet ever dissatisfied; settled, yet ever unsettled, they always enjoy the best of what is, and are the first to find the best of what will be.

(Shakespeare)

Now isn't that a much better way of dealing with age than this:

People of age object too much, consult too long, adventure too little, repent too soon, and content themselves with a mediocrity of success.

(Lord Bacon)

You've heard it before, and it's true—age is a state of mind. I've met many people who seem old at forty, and some who are young at ninety. It seems as though some people were born old, and others never seem to age. The happiest, most satisfied, and most productive people don't give a lot of thought to age. They say they like being where they're at right now, because they wouldn't have been prepared to handle today's problems at an earlier stage of life.

> *John and Mary were avid golfers, even into their eighties. Though they still played well, age was beginning to affect them a bit. John's eyesight was fading, and Mary's memory wasn't so hot. One morning John teed up for the first hole and took a lusty swing. "Now you watch the ball for me, Mary," he said. The sharp crack of the club hitting the ball told him that he had hit a solid drive. "Did you see where it landed, Mary?" he asked excitedly.*
> *"I did," said Mary, "but I forgot."*

You've heard a lot of jokes about the so-called infirmities of age. They might seem less funny as you advance in years, but this story was actually told to me by an eighty-four year old whose eyesight was dimming and whose partner was complaining about her memory. Why were they able to laugh at themselves?

They're humble people, in the sense that "humility" is the ability to see yourself as you really are. They're able to laugh at themselves, the first requisite for humility. They're grateful for what they have, rather than resentful about what they don't have. They're just glad they're still able to play the game, and they're able to appreciate the fact that there are some trade-offs. You might lose some physical ability as you age, but you usually gain something in return.

John, for instance, says, "I can't hit the ball as far as I did when I was younger, but I putt a lot better because I'm not in such a darn hurry." Mary plays better than she did ten years ago. She's taken some lessons, and she's still improving. She could laugh at the joke because she knows that both she and John exaggerate her memory loss. She also knows that when she and John poke fun at each other, it's a sign of their affection.

There's a lot we can learn about aging gracefully from John and Mary's story, and while we're at it, there are some myths about aging that should be dispelled. Let's try to put aging into perspective. It's inevitable, but is there anything you can do about it? Probably more than you think.

First, there's *chronological age.* There's nothing you can do to stop the march of time, so join it. If you're fifty-six now, you'll be fifty-seven a year from now. One way of looking at that is to see that you're one year older. Another way is to see that you've got one more year's experience, so you're one year smarter. You are, that is, if you're learning and growing. Don't be like the job applicant a friend once described to me. "She didn't have thirty year's experience," he said. "She had one year's experience thirty times!"

Remember how you thought about the various stages of life when you were twenty? Most people at that age think that the next fifteen years or so will be a period of growth and success, their lives will reach it's peak between thirty-five and forty, and then it's all downhill. At each stage of life we had both fears and expectations about what the next stage would bring, and experience usually proved our fears to be unfounded. We were almost always more pessimistic than reality deserved.

Age Doesn't Matter Today

A close friend was dying of AIDS, and I knew he didn't have much time left. I visited him regu-

larly, and was always surprised that he was so actively involved in life, as though he was going to be around forever. He must have known what I was thinking, because one day he said, "I've got today, you know. That's all I've ever had, and it's all you've got. If I do something worthwhile or improve myself to-day, then tomorrow, if I get a tomorrow, will be even better. But this day's the only one I can do anything about, so how much time I've got left doesn't matter."

(Forty-four-year-old man)

Of course, we all know that today is the only day we can do anything about, but we still sigh for yesterday and dream of tomorrow. If you can really focus on today, though, then chronological age won't seem so important. If you spend your time regretting the past or worrying about the future instead of living each day to its fullest, you'll cheat yourself. Pope said, "When we are young, we are slavishly employed in procuring something so that we may live comfortably when we are old; and when we are old, we realize that it is too late to live our lives as we proposed." Don't let that happen to you.

There's another way to put aging into perspective, and that's by looking at *physical age.* You can't do much about the progression of chronological age, but you can do quite a bit about physical age. How fast your body ages depends partly on heredity, but you can slow the aging process if you take good care of yourself. Diet, attitude, exercise and adequate rest all contribute to healthy longevity. That's pretty obvious. Some people, though, make the quest for the fountain of youth an obsession, exercising to the point that they do more harm than good. You should accept the fact that your body is aging, and find exercise programs that are appropriate for the condition that you're in.

It's true that your physical abilities diminish with age. What's new about that? It's been happening since you were about twenty-four. If you're smart, your experience will go a long way towards making better use of the abilities you do have.

One of my enduring memories is of working in a general store when I was in high school. I was fifteen years old, 5'11", and weighed 170 pounds. I was in great condition, athletic, with muscles all over the place. My boss was seventy-five, 5'4", and weighed about 120 pounds. Every morning we had to move about twelve sacks of potatoes that weighed 100 pounds each. We'd each move six. Joe was always done before me, and he seemed like he wasn't nearly as exhausted as I was. He had learned how to use leverage, gravity, and how not to use energy he didn't need. He used to say to me, "Don't work hard, work smart." He was using his experience and his knowledge, while I was just using my muscles.

So exercise smart. Stay active, but do what's appropriate for the shape that your body is in. Your golf game may slow down, or you may go from singles to doubles in tennis. Running marathons will change to jogging, then to brisk walks. Keep up with an exercise program, though. Remember, it's not only good for your body, your mind is also more efficient when you're in good physical shape.

No wise man ever wished to be younger.

(Jonathan Swift)

Chronological age is a given. You have some control

over physical aging. But *intellectual aging* is a real positive! Forget the myths about losing your mental acuity as you grow older. It ain't so, at least for most people. There is no reason to expect your intellectual abilities to slow down as the years go by—through your sixties, seventies, or even eighties. What little deterioration might take place is more than made up for by the increased knowledge you gain through experience.

Many people start fretting about memory loss when they can't remember a name or some other detail. While it's true that there will be some slight deterioration of memory as you age, most of the time you are really dealing with information overload. There's simply a lot more information stored in that old computer that we call a brain than there was ten years ago, so it's harder to pull out a single piece of data than it was then. Look at it positively! If your memory's not as sharp as a thirty year old's, it's because you know a lot more than she does! That store of information makes it easier for you to put things in perspective.

> *Like a morning dream, life becomes more and more bright the longer we live, and the reason of everything appears more clear. What has puzzled us before seems less mysterious, and the crooked paths look straighter as we approach the end.*

(Richter)

All of that stored information, along with your experience, makes it easier to learn new things, too. That might be a surprise, because another myth about aging says that it's hard to teach older people. Exactly the opposite is true. Your knowledge and experience give you a great framework within which to evaluate new information. When I was in college and would be flooded with facts in a new course, one of the most difficult tasks would be to try to sort out what was important and what was not. Remember trying to find out what was going to be in the exam? "What's important, teacher?" we'd ask. Now your knowledge and experience do that for you. You almost automatically separate the important from the unimportant. And you discover new things, because something that had no meaning for you earlier in life, suddenly makes a lot of sense. You might ask, "Why should I work to improve myself at this stage of my life? I don't have to work any more." The first stage of your education may have been for the purpose of earning a living. The second stage is for learning how to live.

You have a great deal of control over intellectual aging. It doesn't have to be deterioration at all. If you stay intellectually active and use what you already know, your intellect will not decline, it will improve. You can slow down if you want to, but some of the happiest people I've talked to didn't slow down at all—they sped up. An eighty-four-year-old Ojibway medicine man, describing how busy he was in retirement, said, "I worked at that hospital for forty years. Towards the end, I had four weeks vacation a year. I miss that!"

In your later years, just as when you were young, it's progress that's important. If you learn one new thing each day, you're better off than you were the day before. You still need to feel at the end of the day that you've done something worthwhile, or that you improved yourself. Wouldn't life be dull if you thought there was nothing left to improve?

My dad announced that he had decided to sell the barber shop. I was a little surprised and

somewhat concerned, since it had been keep-
ing him active and he seemed to enjoy it. I
asked him why. "I'm eighty-four," he said, "and
I don't think I'm going to get any better at it. So
I think it's time to try something else!"

(Fifty-four-year-old man)

Spiritual aging is the best news of all. If you let it happen, the coming years can be the most spiritually satisfying period of your life. Age and experience give you the perspective to better understand the meaning of life. When you're younger, you're always looking ahead instead of living each day to its fullest. "People don't live their lives," said Voltaire, "they are always in the *expectation* of living." You have to age to understand the meaning of today.

Expect the Best

Remember the secret of human behavior? *People will behave like you expect them to behave.* If you expect people to treat you differently because you're older, that's what they'll do. If you expect them to respect you for the wisdom and knowledge that have come with experience, you'll get that respect. Now apply that principle to yourself. If you don't expect happiness and fulfillment from your later years, you probably won't get it. Don't short-change yourself. Set your expectations high. Act as though you expect the best to happen, and it's much more likely that it will.

When I was in my forties I had an experience
that taught me how much control I have over
my own happiness. I was going through some
rough times with my family, and I'd wake up
and start the day feeling sorry for myself and
really down. But I was on a job that involved

dealing with people all the time, so it was absolutely essential that I act upbeat and cheerful. I'd force myself to be pleasant even though I felt rotten inside. After a couple of hours of acting cheerful, I'd start feeling that way! I told a friend about it and a couple of days later she handed me a quote by Robert Louis Stevenson that said, "The habit of being happy enables one to be freed from the domination of outward conditions." It still works, and I've been practicing it ever since.

(Seventy-year-old man)

It pays to think positively, even more now than it might have earlier in life. If you project a positive outlook people will respond positively to you. As you look back over your life, focus on what was right, rather than what was wrong. If you had one moment in life when you were what someone needed, you have fulfilled a purpose. If you made one little corner of the world a little less miserable, your life was worthwhile. Someone said that if you do good to others, you double the length of your existence; to look back with pleasure on the good you have done is to live twice.

Two anonymous poets leave us some contrasting thoughts on aging:

Age is a quality of mind;
If you've left your dreams behind,
If hope is cold,
If you no longer look ahead
And ambition fires are dead,
Then, you are old.

In age, you've passed most of the reefs and whirl-pools of life. You have no more enemies left to meet. You've awakened to a new life. Therefore, you are young.

I wish you a happy and fulfilling future, and leave you with these words from Rochefoucald:

> *To understand the world is wiser than to condemn it;*
> *to study the world is better than to shun it.*
> *To use the world is nobler than to abuse it.*
> *To make the world better, lovelier, or happier*
> *is the noblest work of man or woman.*